BEFORE I FORGET

BEFORE I FORGET

A MEMOIR (AND THEN SOME)

ARAM SAROYAN

THREE ROOMS PRESS
New York, NY

Before I Forget: A Memoir (and then some)
by Aram Saroyan

ISBN 978-1-953103-68-0 (trade paperback original)
ISBN 978-1-953103-69-7 (Epub)
Library of Congress Control Number: 2026930283

TRP-123

First Edition

Publication Date: April 21, 2026

BISAC category code
BIO026000 Biography & Autobiography / Personal Memoirs
BIO007000 Biography & Autobiography / Literary Figures
LIT004010 Literary Criticism / Poetry
BIO010000 Biography & Autobiography / Entertainment & Performing Arts

COVER ART:
Copyright © Aram Saroyan

COVER AND INTERIOR DESIGN:
KG Design International

DISTRIBUTED INTERNATIONALLY BY:
Publishers Group West: www.pgw.com
Ingram Content Group: www.ingramcontent.com

PUBLISHED BY:
Three Rooms Press
New York, NY
www.threeroomspress.com
info@threeroomspress.com

For Nancy, with love

What thou lovest well remains,
the rest is dross
What thou lov'st well shall not be rest from thee
What thou lov'st well is thy true heritage

—Ezra Pound

CONTENTS

BEFORE I FORGET

FAMILY PORTRAITS

QUICK NOTES

AT THE BEGINNING OF *DESOLATION ANGELS*, Jack Kerouac is all alone, a fire lookout on a mountain peak in the Pacific Northwest surrounded by mountain stillness on all sides. A practicing if erratic Buddhist—"I'm the Buddha known as the quitter," he quipped once to his friend Gary Snyder—he has an epiphany:

> *"It's me that's changed and done all this and come and gone and complained and hurt and joyed and yelled, not the Void," and so that every time I thought of the void I'd be looking at Mt. Hozomeen (because chair and bed and meadowgrass faced north) until I realized "Hozomeen is the Void—at least Hozomeen means the void to my eyes."*

He eventually comes down from the mountain and joins his friends in San Francisco as the Beat Generation is inaugurated at the famous Gallery Six reading in the mid-1950s when Allen Ginsberg first read "Howl"—Kerouac in the audience with a wine bottle shouting "Go!"

The novel, the middle one of his three masterworks (between *On the Road* and *Big Sur*), is a huge chronicle of earthly comings and goings, but it's the stillness on the mountain at the beginning that sets the book's compass—Kerouac carrying it in himself through the human panorama into which he journeys when he comes down from the mountain.

It's this double vision, I think, that distinguishes the artist from the journalist or the historian, even while Kerouac plays both those roles too over the course of the book—a deeper vision running through everything he sees, the still center of the hurricane that is also the hurricane. He's the fumbling guy—the charming troubled mortal Kerouac could be in his prose—and at the same time the steadfast mountain, unmoved by the sound and fury of an individual destiny.

In high school I read the treatise *Art* by Clive Bell, a Capricorn paperback with a palm tree rendered in quick green brush strokes on the cover. I was looking for an overview, which the title promised and which the book delivered in the form of a two-word catch-all: Significant Form. That's what distinguished a work of art, Clive Bell stated. I didn't really understand what he meant, but I got it at some level that had to do with finding certain abstract paintings satisfying—like the works of Serge Poliakoff, for example—without understanding why.

In the early days of television, the mid-1950s, when I was seven or eight years old, I remember watching an episode of a weekly drama and hearing background music that affected me powerfully. It seemed to me the most beautiful melody. Some time later I found out it was Gershwin's "Someone to Watch Over Me."

For 15 years I taught at USC's Master of Professional Writing program and had many interesting, beguiling students scarcely any of whom became writers. The time they spent will no doubt serve them well in one context or another. But MFA programs, cash cows for universities, in effect promote an idea about art that is fundamentally false. It would be harmless most likely except that having so large a number of "certified" artists and writers tends to create a watered-down version of art itself.

As very young siblings my younger sister Lucy and I used to take baths together. Facing each other at opposite ends of the tub, we would slowly lower our bodies into the water—always just the right temperature—and slowly enunciate to each other in unison, "Oh, my *fa-vor-ite* water."

Storytelling, all art maybe, can be a way of whistling in the dark, trying to reassure oneself and perhaps others that what is happening isn't just terror and chaos. The cave drawings at Lascaux were perhaps an attempt to "domesticate" the wild beasts roaming outside. Give the terror a name or a drawing and its scale is at least to some degree reduced.

My early childhood was a mix of privilege and violent misery that tore the family apart twice by the time I was eight. For a child it was alternately wonderful—in the early years—and devastating—just a little later. By the time I was eight, when Lucy and I shared a little bedroom in my mother's one-bedroom apartment on Olympic Boulevard in Beverly Hills, I had a strong impulse to take the bull by the horns and initiate a sort of talking cure. In the darkness of the bedroom before we fell asleep I would imitate school "assemblies" with an announcement or a song, and ask Lucy to add her own contribution, which she sometimes did. It gave me, and maybe Lucy once in a while too, a sense of business as usual, not total chaos.

When I was ten or eleven, living in a ranch house in Pacific Palisades with my mother and sister, I found the blue and yellow UCLA colors a perfect combination.

* * *

The first work by Richard Brautigan I ever read was in a little mimeographed magazine called *Sum*, edited by the Canadian poet Fred Wah, published in New Mexico and mailed to me in New York probably because I was editing my own little magazine, *Lines*, and we were on each other's comp copy lists. This would have been 1964 or early 1965.

In one issue there were a couple of very short stories by a writer named Richard Brautigan and they stood out for two reasons. The first was that they were flat-out wonderful. In one of them a woman was sunbathing on the beach and taking her own temperature. My memory may have the scene wrong but the piece had a kind of sunny languor. It made the scene come alive inside you.

The second reason the stories stood out was that both of them—and neither filled up a single page—included a formal copyright notice with the copyright logo, the year and the author's name. I had never read or seen anything by Brautigan before but the message was clear: Richard Brautigan was a delightful writer and Richard Brautigan knew it.

In the classic Alfred Hitchcock films of the 1950s—*Vertigo, North by Northwest, Rear Window*—he captures the ambient sounds of American urban and suburban neighborhoods more accurately than I've heard in any other films.

When my father took Lucy and me to Europe the summer—I was 13 and Lucy 11—we stayed for two weeks at a hotel in Athens and from the street you could look up at the Acropolis on a hill above the city. The classic balance and beauty of it had the effect of instantaneous reassurance.

The same summer when I saw the Plaza San Marco in Venice it struck me as the most beautiful place I'd ever seen. The great breadth and depth of the piazza at the end of which stood St. Marks Church with blue lapis lazuli mosaic in its façade was beyond words.

I collect pennies in a roughly sculpted clay cup my younger daughter made years ago in an art class in elementary school. It's painted yellow inside and out, with a purple flower on a green stalk on one side and a red flower on a green stalk on the other. It fits easily into my hand. For several years now I've used it to keep pennies in from the loose change I accumulate. When it's filled to the brim it holds around 150 pennies, enough to fill 3 penny rolls. When I get about five dollars worth of penny rolls I take them to the bank to exchange for singles or a five dollar bill.

There's some kind of primitive satisfaction in taking something as non-negotiable as a penny, which once had the value of a nickel, say, and by accumulation, turning it into something that has value.

HERITAGE

THE YOUNGEST AND ONLY AMERICAN-BORN CHILD of an Armenian immigrant family, my father grew up and came of age on the West Coast, a writer out of the loop of the New York literary scene that might have given his career a jump start. Among his correspondence now at Stanford's Special Collections Library is a letter from 1928, the year he turned 20, from Clifton Fadiman, then a young editor at Simon & Schuster.

Fadiman praises a group of stories he'd received and says he would be very interested in seeing a novel. It would be six more years, however, before William Saroyan would make his national breakthrough with his famous story "The Daring Young Man on the Flying Trapeze." It was 1934, the depths of the Depression, and the story, with its personal as well as its national resonance, tells of a young writer in San Francisco who over the course of a day succumbs to starvation and dies. At 26, my father had at last hit the note that would bring him not just acceptance, but national and quickly international fame.

By the time the story appeared, the deferred hour of reckoning in a career that in another less determined writer might not have dawned at all, he was already a stylist, master of a prose light years beyond all but one or two of his most accomplished contemporaries. The final two paragraphs of the story, about the last moments of the young writer's life, read:

> *He became drowsy and felt a ghastly illness coming over his blood, a feeling of nausea and disintegration. Bewildered, he stood beside his bed, thinking there is nothing to do but sleep. Already he felt himself making great strides through the fluid of the earth, swimming away to the beginning. He fell face down upon the bed, saying, I ought first at least to give the coin to some child. A child could buy any number of things with a penny.*
>
> *Then swiftly, neatly, with the grace of the young man on the trapeze, he was gone from his body. For an eternal moment he was all things at once: the bird, the fish, the rodent, the reptile, and man. An ocean of print undulated endlessly and darkly before him. The city burned. The herded crowd rioted. The earth circled away, and knowing that he did so, he turned his face to the empty sky and became dreamless, unalive, perfect.*

Here was an Armenian-American writer—and Armenians of his day in Fresno were looked down on—destined to become an international literary sensation, quickly eclipsing the Fresno fame of his uncle, Aram Saroyan, the younger brother of his mother, Takoohi.

Uncle Aram, as he was widely known with a sort of "Godfather" resonance in the Fresno Armenian community, represented the first American success of the Saroyan clan. Assimilation or not, scorned Armenian or not—and houses in

Fresno were posted with for sale and rental signs that read "no Armenians" in smaller print—the man commanded. A criminal lawyer and the owner of vineyards, he was a powerful physical presence, he had money, he was smart, and he didn't take no for an answer.

What an urgency to assimilate may not allow for are those issues and particular concerns identified with a culture. When these were taken up in turn by my father, he encountered loud derision from his mother's brother, the male role-model in his immediate orbit, after his father Armenak Saroyan's death at 37 when my father was not yet three years old.

"You want to write?" Aram shouted at the adolescent Willie Saroyan after he confided his aspiration. "Learn to write checks!"

That my father eventually succeeded in his literary endeavor to such unprecedented a degree that he became the most famous Armenian of his time, and perhaps in that day the most famous Armenian *of all time*, had a powerful effect on his extended family at large.

From the beginning, I was identified as the son of a famous American writer, though hardly known that way to myself. I remember one afternoon getting on a school bus in Manhattan, where I was going to kindergarten or the first grade, and having kids point me out to one another. At some point it was suggested that it had something to do with my parents getting divorced. I didn't know what "divorce" meant, but could see it was news.

Fame in effect reverses the whole assimilation scenario. Celebrity becomes a kind of nation unto itself, one which bestows a special passport on its subject and his family, all of whom know the world a bit differently than it's known by others. For my father, a flamboyant literary figure of the thirties and forties, fame involved both licenses and personal and professional liabilities. But as he got older, having passed his golden moment and becoming a parent and then an ex-husband, his persona changed, and some of my fondest memories of him have to do with this change.

At his height, as the new American wizard of the short story and then quickly the enfant terrible of the American theater, Saroyan became for the 1930s a literary figure comparable to what F. Scott Fitzgerald had been for the 1920s. He was, on the testimony of many, a socially dominant figure, young, handsome, loud, funny and, to use one of his favorite words, swift. Even after his glory days had long passed, he retained that accelerated temper—he was forever moving somewhere, walking, talking, looking, exclaiming at things—and he was the father of a son whose own temper, while similar in certain ways, was generally a study in contrast. I don't have my father's speed, and my temper is less exhibitionistic, though not immune to theatrics. What moves me in my memories of him are the times at which, I see now, he recognizably lowered his own natural volume to take in his son's quieter register. He was interested, in a word, which can't be said of every father. We spent time together; we discussed many things. The child of a broken marriage that left both parties embittered, I realized rather late in life that, unlike many of my male friends, I actually *knew* my father; I laughed with him, I saw him in good times and bad. If he could be impossible—and he could be—knowing him was nonetheless a great gift of my life.

Unlike his immediate predecessor Fitzgerald, who was gone at forty-four, and his successor, Kerouac, gone at forty-seven—he was a survivor. My father died at seventy-two, and in his later years, while no longer the movie-star figure of his youth, he had recovered his literary balance in a series of memoirs and a late series of stories where he's back at the top of his form.

Having found vocation early on, long before fame found *him*, he had its support later in his life when much else had been lost, including that fame, his ill-fated marriage, and two children from whom in his last years he was estranged. Nonetheless, he went on writing, went on making his drawings and water-colors, and being William Saroyan in the larger literary community that never forgot him. It was an imperishable inheritance he had discovered, and it stood him in good stead in his lean later years. While he'd known a public apotheosis as a writer that only a handful in his century achieved, and the passing of which was fatally punishing for a seeming majority of them, he lived on, perhaps not so unhappily, in the way of an artisan, ever engaged by his art and craft.

In time, too, he came to disdain the particulars of the society that had given him such a wild ride. "We live in a bullshit culture," he declared in a quiet, bemused tone after he'd done the round of television talk shows upon the publication of one of his later memoirs and seen the sales multiply geometrically. He was a beneficiary of the Oprah Club, as it were, before it existed, but he had known bigger sales before the advent of television and the new wrinkle wasn't about to rock his world.

By the time I came to know him, then, leaving aside the bitterness he harbored toward my mother, he was a seasoned realist who had toughened and deepened over the years. He imparted to me his love for genuine art in all its forms, and when we were on good terms, it was something we could return to with pleasure.

At the same time, his temper had been damaged by his experience and he turned away from the larger life he might have known in his later years, perhaps knowing that he was constitutionally unequal to it. While a virile, attractive man virtually to the end of his life, he didn't engage in any serious relationship after his double-marriage to and double-divorce from my mother, and now I think of this as a sad but in certain ways admirable realism. There may even have been in him a concern for the vulnerability of any partner he might have taken on—and there was never a shortage of willing women—perhaps now knowing himself to be more or less inflexibly a loner.

My mother, meanwhile, had found another life, with another man who seven years along in their marriage became a movie-star, and yet she remained embittered, and, I believe, was ultimately more engaged by what had happened with my father in her youth than Bill, who had no significant new life afterwards, was himself.

2

When I go back in time to that young woman of 1951 who walked out on their second marriage, and for the ten years that followed, I see in Carol a besieged, brave woman warrior of her day, and know that I owe her courage real homage. She wasn't William Saroyan, the famous writer, and yet she stood up to him, broke away, and created a new life for herself and her two children.

She had nerve, she had guts—and this must have been tough for my father, who knew her to be undisciplined, unschooled (she had graduated from Dalton in New York but never seriously considered college), a "party girl" who would now raise his two children. And this was my father in an uncharacteristically solemn phase of his life. For some years he seemed to become a stiff, unsmiling shadow of his former loud, boisterous, laughing self. He was in his forties now, to be sure, while his ex-wife was still in her twenties.

I have to be grateful for my mother's ballsy affront to the received wisdom that she was the lucky wife of a great man. If she had stayed with Bill, she could have only receded into depression and the horizons of my own life would have also darkened and diminished. I owe those larger lighter horizons to her.

My knowledge of Carol's side of the family amounts to far less than what I know of my father's side. I know that the Russian Jewish Brophman family arrived in the early years of the last century. My maternal grandmother, Rosheen

Brophman, was born in Yidinitz near Kiev in 1908, the same year Bill was born in Fresno, but grew up in an apartment in Gramercy Park. She had a love affair at 16 and, having gotten pregnant, was thrown out of the house by her mother—all of this according to the sketchy history I've pieced together over the years. She became a millinery model and a Ziegfeld Follies chorus girl; and during those years Carol lived in foster homes, eventually finding a permanent home with a woman named Genevieve Laragay in Paterson, New Jersey.

"What is this orphan crap," Rosheen complained over the years, and most strenuously when Carol's memoir, *Among the Porcupines,* was published. "She wasn't an orphan. She stayed with a very nice woman for a little while."

Carol talked about Rosheen quite affectionately one afternoon. She'd phoned me from Minneapolis, where Walter was making *Grumpier Old Men.*

"She's done something really terrible," she said about Grandma, who now was living in a Manhattan rest home. "She's become nice. I brought her her favorite perfume, and as a trick I'll sing one of her favorite old songs, and then I'll pretend I've forgotten the words, and she'll come right in with them. She remembers."

As we talked I realized Carol was quite preoccupied with death herself.

"At a certain point, you know you're going down," she said. "I mean you're not going to turn around. Do you know what I mean?"

I imagined I knew something of what she was saying, but in my fifties it took the form of a sort of diffuse poignancy, whereas I knew she was speaking in part about the physical pain of her arthritis.

"'I wish I would just die,'" she said Rosheen told her.

"But I told her," Carol said. "'Oh, no, you're not going to do that, because I'm going to come with you.' And she said, 'Well, that would be nice.'"

Rosheen was beautiful, and the marriage she eventually made had more than incidentally to do with that. Her husband, Charles Marcus, a German Jewish scientist and Vice President at Bendix Aviation, was an extraordinary man, a lover of Mozart and a great purveyor of civilization within the family. At the same time, he didn't believe he was good looking, although he was a tall authoritative figure and after his separation from Rosheen had many women friends.

Charles Marcus was an important family figure as I was growing up. He was a man who wasn't rushing, while both my father and mother seemed, albeit in different ways, to be breathless in their circumstance of the moment. This was a style I distrusted, and I was reassured by the fact that my grandfather, clearly in full possession of his faculties, wasn't in a rush. After my parents' second divorce, and his own separation from Rosheen (the two never divorced), he was a regular Sunday guest in our house both before and after Carol married Walter.

Late in his life, during the 1980s, I remember him telling me that a sense of humor dissolved the dark clouds of one's life like a gentle healing rain. He lived on into his 90s at the Beverly Wilshire Hotel, where Carol would have dinner with him each week at The Pink Turtle.

Carol and Walter both found in Charles Marcus, I think, an important paternal support, a man of great learning—in his seventies he invented the laser fire extinguisher that was utilized on the first flight to the moon—who represented an intellectual height of achievement of their own race.

Rosheen had a simplicity about her that I came to cherish over the years. She spoke her mind clearly, and wasn't possessed of the same feminine wiles I identify with Carol. She took great pride in having given her daughters, Carol and her younger half-sister Elinor, a good start in the world by means of her marriage to Charles Marcus. She was also very proud of the fact that she was the wife of so distinguished a man, and ran a large household in Manhattan that became well known to the high-rollers with whom she and her daughters became friends: a group that included Errol Flynn, Truman Capote, Artie Shaw, Lee Wiley, Gloria Vanderbilt and Oona O'Neill, among others.

When Carol and Walter gave a garden party in Pacific Palisades for Charlie and Oona Chaplin, Rosheen was appalled that caviar was served out of buckets.

"That's nouveau riche," she said. "Rich people don't do that kind of extravagant display. No matter how much money you have, you make it something special."

Rosheen invoked this sense of social propriety while at the same time keeping her own extended family at a distance. In her later years she seemed to reconsider her denial of their place in her life, at least when she wasn't preoccupied with Carol and her social profile. Gradually I became aware of cousins in Oregon and California and New Jersey whom I'd never known. Occasionally I'd discover Rosheen in the kitchen or the bedroom in her Park Avenue apartment entertaining one of these relatives, to whom I'd then be introduced.

MY OWN AVEDON

I FIRST MET HIM IN 1956 at the annual Christmas day party given by Sidney and Gloria Vanderbilt Lumet in their Gracie Square penthouse. Gloria had two sons by Leopold Stokowski, Stan and Chris, who were a little younger than I was—seven or eight to my thirteen—and with the younger children given the run of the brothers' bedroom, as well as the adults holding forth in the living room, I was a bit of a fish out of water.

I ended up sitting at the side of the living room on a sofa and was joined by a slender handsome man who, while obviously an adult, had such an easy, undaunting manner that he was like an impossibly well-mannered contemporary. We started to play a game called Ghost, a word game, and talked as we played. I remember him saying at one point that he himself was Jewish, which seemed very frank of him, although what the significance of it was, wasn't very clear to me. As it turned out, he had trouble figuring out my word. He asked if the word could be "carrot," once, and then again. Then he got it—"actor."

As evening came on my mother wanted to leave with me and Lucy, and I said goodbye to the man in the midst of another game of Ghost, in which I was now trying to figure out his word. Leaving soon himself, he said that I should call him when I got home and we'd finish the game on the phone.

In the taxi home, Carol told me that the man was Richard Avedon, one of the most famous photographers in the world. Although I was an enthusiastic member of the Photography Club at Robert F. Wagner Junior High, I didn't know his work. When we got home, I called him and struggled for a while longer with his word, and then had an epiphany when I thought the word might be "carrot" and realized that his word, too, was "actor."

I was a kid who had been uprooted from a few years of a semi-idyllic middle-class childhood in a ranch house in Pacific Palisades into this strange nerve-center, Manhattan. For an adolescent boy it wasn't the optimal environment and I was upset and angry. At the same time I felt an urgency to make contact in some outside arena; outside my own household, that is, with my 32-year-old mother and my 11-year-old sister—but my father no longer living nearby.

A few days after the Christmas party I brought up to Carol the idea that maybe I could volunteer to work for Avedon and learn more about photography. She said she thought it was an interesting idea and eventually I worked up the courage to call him. My mother could be very helpful in these kinds of matters and in the meantime had eased the way with Avedon for my phone call.

Thus started my after-school job at the studio, which was on 49th Street and Third Avenue over a green-shuttered steak house called Manny Wolf's. Dick hired me as an "apprentice" and paid me $10 a week so that, as he put it, he would feel free to yell at me if I goofed up. What had struck me most about him at the Christmas party was that he seemed to be happy in a way that I'd never seen before in an adult.

Going after school to the studio, it was as if the theater of a brilliant new world opened its curtains. I swept floors, loaded Dick's alternate Rollie during shooting sessions, and eventually—mentored by Avedon's young assistant, Hiro Wakabayashi, a recent émigré from Japan who would become the renowned photographer Hiro—began to develop film and print contact sheets.

Once I arrived in the afternoon and began learning and doing my assigned chores, I seldom saw Dick other than during a shooting session, where he took photographs at a phenomenal speed. He would hand me a camera in which he'd shot the 12 exposures and I'd hand him back the other Rollie with a new roll of film so he could take more or less continuous shots of his subject. And it often became a close race between me emptying and reloading one camera and the time it took for Dick to take 12 new shots with the other. He usually had music on the stereo, timely and/or hit music, especially during a fashion session. Johnny Mathis had recently surfaced and he liked an album in which Mathis covered songs from *West Side Story*, which had just opened on Broadway.

"Isn't this the sexiest thing you've ever heard?" he said to the fashion coordinator Polly Mellon one afternoon before a session.

With the Rollie fixed to a tripod by one of his assistants and the lights set with the signature white roll of paper as the backdrop, he would kick-start a session, it seemed to me, by taking photographs mostly for the purpose of putting his subject at ease, to establish an ambience of permission and approval. Then as the subject grew progressively freer, more relaxed and comfortable, he no longer needed to flatter or cajole by means of the shutter and would now be tracking to *get* the photograph.

During the fashion shoots, the fashion coordinator, along with the people from the magazine, the ad company and/or the product line, all stood behind or beside him as he worked. As he took the photographs, the music on full blast, he would exclaim each time he clicked the shutter: "sensational!...fantastic!...terrific!"—a dynamic that ramped up the energy and brought the best out of the models, and thus a practical, not to say pragmatic technique. Which isn't to say that Dick didn't mean each exclamation; I think he did. It was like a shamanistic protocol, and if his energy and commitment faltered, the whole house of cards might have fallen down. In a word, it was his job—the craftspeople standing beside him no less susceptible to the atmosphere than the models—but it was also a gift.

Early on during my time working in the studio, there was a big shoot in color with Marilyn Monroe portraying a variety of previous American glamour girls: Clara Bow, Jean Harlow, Lillian Russell and so on—with stage-sets and props rather than the signature white backdrop. Marilyn was in the studio for several days for Dick to photograph her wearing different costumes, make-up and wigs in the various settings. At one point in a session where there was semi-nudity she discreetly noted my presence and Dick dispatched me to another part of the studio.

She was, of course, a major icon in my adolescent mind, although to be honest she looked too much like my mother to be quite the sexual lodestar I know she was for many of my contemporaries. I was introduced to her in passing the first day, and when Arthur Miller, whom she'd recently married, visited the studio, she stopped and introduced me.

"Honey," she said, "this is Bill Saroyan's son."

I'd been a member of the first sixth grade graduating class of the brand new Marquez Knolls Elementary School in Pacific Palisades. At the ceremony we sang the school song, which, the obligatory piety aside, renders quite accurately the lovely, semi-rural environs:

Marquez Knolls we offer thee
More than the pledge of our loyalty
Deep in our hearts we hold so dear
The blue of the sky and the air so clear
The ocean that reaches other lands
The greens of the canyons, the golden sands
Our love do we give
As long as we live Marquez Knolls

A year and a half later, leaving Wagner Junior High at 3:00, just outside the front doors on 76th Street between Third and Second Avenues, I saw two boys confronting each other.

The smaller one, about my size, had his hand stuck in the top of his zippered jacket. In a thick New York accent he said to a much larger boy, one I thought of as good-natured and humorous: "You take one more step and I'm gonna put a big nail in the middle of your head."

In another moment the larger kid had him down on the pavement and was banging his head on the sidewalk.

The next day during PE on the 75th Street side of the school where there was a paved play area, I told Mr. Licht, my home room teacher, a kindly portly man who taught Science, about the incident. I'd meanwhile gathered that the threat about the nail referred to a zip gun.

We lived on the fourth floor of a five-story apartment building, 53 East 93rd Street, near the corner of Madison Avenue. A thin buff-colored building with rounded corners, it had been featured eponymously in a spy movie, *The House on 92nd Street* (sic). On the opposite side of the street, directly across from us, was a mansion where the Broadway impresario Billy Rose lived. (Years later the building housed an alcoholic rehab facility where John Cheever spent time near the end of his life).

That night in my bedroom at the back of our two-bedroom apartment—my mother slept on a foldout couch in the living room, while Lucy slept in the other little bedroom next door to mine—I was seized with a fear that the boy with the zip gun would find out I had told on him and would come in my bedroom window, overlooking the backyards of the buildings on 94th Street, and kill me. I needed my dad or some other man to put this hysterical fear to rest, but no such person was available as my mind raced. Eventually I fell asleep and the next morning discovered myself in one piece and got up and went back to school.

I needed a better camera than our family Brownie, and eventually got a Minolta Autocord, a good Japanese knock-off of a Rollie at about a third the price. During those days I was likely to carry an envelope with one of my photographs in it, ready-to-hand documentary proof, in case it was needed, of my new identity as a photographer. The necessity for this surely went back to the seismic shift from the Southern California suburb I'd known to this labyrinth, Manhattan, made up of concrete and steel and glass.

Instead of Little League, which I'd loved, there were now movie houses and theaters. On East 86th Street, our local movie street, along with the two big RKO and Loews first-run movie houses, there was a small repertory house called The Grande, and once I knew it was there it became a luxurious touchstone—I could find its little ad in The New York Times—likely to be showing a double feature of classic films every week.

Courtesy of the studio, I got to attend a screening of the musical *Funny Face*, starring Fred Astaire and Audrey Hepburn, with a score by the Gershwins—the musical in which an Avedon-like photographer, Astaire, shoots the Paris collection with his new discovery, Hepburn, as his model. Dick had been an advisor on the film. To see that movie and at the same time be Avedon's apprentice was a kind of ecstasy, the only comparable experience being a sixth row center seat my mother somehow got me for a performance of *Damn Yankees*, starring Gwen Verdon and Ray Walston, at the Winter Garden theater on Broadway.

The actress Lee Grant once described Carol as a "big white cat," and her friend Peggy Lloyd said that she carried her own kingdom around with her. What went into this impression, it seemed to me as a member of her household, were hours upon hours of a state of semi-consciousness. It was as if her nature as perceived by others only occurred under the pressure of a crisis, or a social or a work commitment. Otherwise she appeared to be recharging a battery that was perpetually running low.

A foster child until she was eight years old, when Rosheen married Charles Marcus, Carol moved from the home of her foster parent, Genevieve Laragay, in Paterson, into her mother and stepfather's big Park Avenue apartment, seeming to take the change of venue as her birthright. At Dalton School she was both popular and feared, navigating the Upper East Side social waters with a built-in radar that wouldn't suffer fools kindly.

By the time she was attending the debutante tea dances of the period, with the war already on in Europe, her two best friends were Oona O'Neill, the daughter of Eugene O'Neill, and Gloria Vanderbilt, in a media spotlight from the age of ten as the "Poor Little Rich Girl" at the center of a custody battle between her mother and her aunt, Gertrude Whitney.

Popular as she was at the dances, though, trading off blue-blood dance partners like Stevie Hopkins (the son of FDR's cabinet minister Harry Hopkins), Kingdon Gould and Fletcher Godfrey, there was an unspoken understanding that these Manhattan scions would never marry outside their class, and Carol's Jewish mother and step-father ruled her out.

And who was William Saroyan, after all, but the son of Armenian immigrants who had made literary high modernism funny and easy in the middle of the dark hours of the Depression? By all accounts, the meeting of these two self-invented Americans set off sparks. Then too, for Carol marrying the famous writer was a way around the social hierarchy of WASP New York, her standing now legitimized.

After the war, settling into a domestic partnership and motherhood, neither of which she was prepared for, she encountered a self-made tyrant and compulsive gambler who was then experiencing a shift in the zeitgeist that would move him from the literary center to the margins.

Carol's divorce from Bill, handled for her by Jerry Geisler, the high-powered Beverly Hills divorce lawyer, yielded a mere $400 a month in child support. Her motives for accepting this settlement when Geisler advised her that she could do much better attest to a powerful instinct to carve out a life of her own. As she once explained it, she didn't want to end up the sort of "alimony queen" who doesn't have to lift a finger for the rest of her days and ends up a testy, querulous eccentric.

Then too, she was still in her twenties, and, as she had proven *before* she met Bill, possessed a kind of social genius.

Before leaving the Palisades she had written a novella, *The Secret in the Daisy*, which was published by Random House after our arrival in the city. On arrival, too, she had already been hired to play the supporting role of the secretary and to understudy Jayne Mansfield in George Axelrod's Broadway comedy, *Will Success Spoil Rock Hunter?* One of the lead roles was played by Walter and the two would get married a few years later.

"I fell in love with your mother's past," Bill told me, long after the storm of their relationship had subsided. I gathered he meant the little foster child who then went on to invent herself as a beautiful blond combination of Jean Harlow and Gertrude Stein.

Dick and his wife Evelyn, an elegant blond woman in contrast to Carol's faux-naif sex-bomb, lived with their infant son, Johnny, on Park Avenue. When Carol and Lucy and I visited one night for dinner, I was dazzled by the entry with its red-and-white, large-squared, checker-board linoleum floor. It was flamboyance, color and control all at the same time. Here was someone who had mastered the world, I thought.

2

Even in my early memories of him, my father seems older, if not exactly old. Partly it had to do with the age difference between Carol and Bill, 16 years—and that they'd married when she was 18 and he was 34. At that moment, February of 1943, he was arguably the most famous writer in America, the literary hero of the Great Depression for his ebullient, devil-may-care stories (*The Daring Young Man on the Flying Trapeze*) and plays (*The Time of Your Life*). *The Human Comedy*, his first novel, which portrayed the stateside war effort, was simultaneously an MGM movie starring Mickey Rooney, the number one box-office star in America, and a Book of the Month Club main selection with an advance order of 350,000 copies.

After a grim army experience as a member of the film unit posted to London—he was constitutionally incapable of being a good soldier—he returned to his young wife, whom he scarcely knew, and their infant son, and tried to recapture his literary rhythm and worldly standing in a post-war America that had left the Depression behind. If his early insouciance in the face of economic disaster had once seemed charming and restorative, he was now accused of wearing "rose-colored glasses," a sentimentalist. His anti-war novel, *The Adventures of Wesley Jackson*, written while in London and held up by the publisher until the war was over, was reviewed on the front page of *The New York Times Book Review* by his erstwhile friend from the film unit, Irwin Shaw. "Saroyan forgives the Germans

Dachau and Belson without blinking an eye," Shaw wrote, "but he cannot forgive the Sergeant who assigned him to K.P. in New York City," a shamelessly willful misreading of the book.

I believe he was now grappling with an ongoing depression that would never entirely loosen its hold on him. "We tend toward melancholy," he said to me in my thirties as if shedding light on our shared natures. But while I've known depression in my time, when I saw him again after Carol's move with Lucy and me to New York, he seemed to carry a gray aura with him. He would check into a room he had occupied years before at the Great Northern Hotel on West 57th Street, a remnant of his glory days—he'd written *The Time of Your Life* there in six days—as if to revive the golden moment.

Taking summer custody of us, as decreed by the divorce agreement, he arranged to take Lucy and me to Europe for the summer of 1957, booking first class passage for the three of us on the trans-Atlantic cruise ship of the Italian line, the *MS Vulcania.*

As a going-away present, Dick gave me a box of black & white film, 20 rolls of Kodak PlusEx, and a box of 20 Kodak Ektachrome color rolls. The cruise ship itinerary after the Atlantic crossing included six-hour stops at a series of Adriatic and Mediterranean port cities: Palermo, Naples, Venice, Patras, etc., and Pop encouraged me to get out into the streets with my camera and photograph kids. Since I was still a kid myself, my subjects could engage with the camera without worrying about an adult figure behind it, and the results, most of which I wouldn't see until I was back in New York, turned out luckier than I could have predicted.

That fall, I started as a high school freshman at Trinity, the venerable all-boys private school where the uniform was a blue blazer with the Trinity crest on the pocket. The school day began each morning with chapel service, after which I encountered a schedule of classes far in advance of my academic background and abilities: Latin, Algebra, English, Civics and Ancient History. I was in over my head. My homeroom teacher, Frank Smith, an Oxford graduate who taught Latin, took a kindly bemused interest in my situation.

Poor in Latin from day one, I decided to cheat on a "pop quiz" I knew was coming by writing answers on a sheet I folded to a size I could cup in my palm and rotate for the answers and then took a seat at a desk in the back row of our class.

Writing the questions on the black board, Mr. Smith would turn around from time to time to observe us as we began writing our answers. When he did this at one point he looked directly at me in the back row with my crib sheet cupped in my hand. I looked at him as he looked at me and the impending disaster ticked off in my mind: I would be called out of class, taken to the principal Mr. Riddleburger's office, Carol would be phoned, and eventually Bill in California.

Mr. Smith registered in full this disastrous error on my part and then turned back to the board and continued to write out the questions. I got rid of the wadded up piece of paper and wrote whatever answers I could manage to conjure up. The next day at the end of the class he returned our pop quizzes to us as we left for the next class. Handing me mine with its failing grade, he said pointedly, "Now, boy, be very careful how you go about this, do you understand?"

"Yes, sir."

Even at the time, I couldn't help admiring how he handled it while effectively nipping my cheating career in the bud.

Meanwhile, the European rolls of black & white and the color transparencies, which were developed in a couple of days at the studio and the color lab we used, provided a kind of excitement and sense of accomplishment I'd never known. Hiro was taken with several shots on the contact sheets, which he made prints of in the darkroom after work, showing me how to "burn in" certain parts of an image and crop out or lighten other parts, his hands holding back the enlarger's light from the photo paper.

Dick arranged for me to meet with Marvin Israel, the Art Director at *Seventeen* magazine, who designed a beautiful two-page layout of eight photographs that ran in the January 1958 issue of the magazine under the heading "Lens on Europe." I was asked to write several lines below or above each of the eight photographs he chose.

Carol tried to help me with these but when the proofs arrived she grew testy. "You can't use the word 'located' in this one," she said.

"Why?" I asked.

"Because it's the kind of word used by someone like John Foster Dulles. You sound like a government bureaucrat."

Still, the layout won an Art Directors Award for both Marvin and me, and when I went to pick up the certificate at the mid-town exhibit one afternoon, I was greeted with surprise as a prodigy.

3

MORE OR LESS INEVITABLY I FAILED my freshman year at Trinity, and the following year was sent away to boarding school to repeat it. By the time I returned to Trinity as a sophomore, my interest in photography had waned, to be gradually replaced by writing. The next time I saw Dick again in an intimate setting was in 1975 with Lucy, who had become his friend. He was now living in a loft-like apartment on the floor above his studio in a building in the East 70s. He and Evelyn had separated, and his son John had grown up and would eventually become a writer and a devotee of the Dalai Lama.

I'd just published my first prose book, an autobiographical novel remembering the sixties called *The Street*, which Dick had responded warmly to, and our meeting now seemed to have more to do with the book than with our past. All his life Dick had a fondness for writers, forming friendships with Harold Brodkey and Renata Adler, among others, and as he talked that night it seemed to me that his autobiographical candor was a reflection of his literary engagement.

He had discovered that a man who bore a physical resemblance to him had been impersonating him in New York, picking up women by pretending to be Richard Avedon. He contacted the man, met with him and did studio portraits of them both in similar poses. The shots he showed us were from the waist up and he and the man, both shirtless, had unbuckled their belts and the top button of their trousers. I said something about their semi-nakedness.

"Yes," he said. "Because what I probably *really* wanted to see was our cocks."

It was a strange tableau: Lucy, Dick and I in his luxurious cave in New York, with books piled in stacks on the floor, delving into this solipsistic preoccupation of the moment.

Rolling Stone had recently run an entire issue of Avedon portraits, "The Family," a gallery of famous Americans from President Ford to Abbie Hoffman, from Henry Kissinger to Andy Warhol and the Factory crowd.

With the advent of the sixties, I'd gotten a certain psychological footing for the first time, I felt, and was secretly a little proprietary about Dick's appropriation of *Rolling Stone*, a venue that originated in my generation. I also entertained private reservations about his grasp of the period. I'd been living with Gailyn and our two very young daughters for the past several years in Bolinas, and while we were actual sixties people, I felt, we weren't on his radar in thinking about the period because we weren't famous.

A social movement that made not a chosen few of us famous but rather bestowed fame on a generation en masse, was, for me, the son of a famous writer and the step-son of a movie-star, a made-to-order boon—which is to say that the essence of the sixties, as I saw it, was communal and not hierarchical. But Dick wasn't about to buy that, if in fact it occurred to him, and his portraits from our generation were of the usual suspects as decreed by *Time* magazine.

In May of 1977, less than a year after the birth of our third and last child, our son Armenak, Dick called from Los Angeles. He and Lucy, who now lived in Beverly Hills, were going to visit us in Bolinas. Having completed some work in L.A., he wanted to take a few days off before heading back to New York.

"Don't worry about anything," he said. "I'm so cool with this."

We were surprised and flattered by the call, and arranged accommodations for Dick and Lucy in Inverness. At the same time, Gailyn and I were exhausted young parents, with a new infant in our midst, and uncertain how we would negotiate our impromptu guests.

Dick rented a car at the airport and he and Lucy were soon at our ramshackle house on Hawthorn Road at the crest of a hill on the Bolinas mesa. In his early fifties now, he still possessed the same infectious combination of energy and attentiveness. We all spent several days together, talking, having meals, and driving around West Marin County during the chilly spring.

I'd recently finished writing a review of his new book of photographs, *Portraits*, which he'd sent us, and commented in it on a portrait of Truman Capote in striking contrast to the portrait of him in Dick's first book, *Observations*, for which Capote had done the text. While the earlier portrait shows a beaming, radiant young writer, in the later one Capote appears to be in the throes of some acute form of dyspepsia. Was this Avedon acting on behalf of high-powered friends wounded by the revelations in the excerpts from Capote's *Answered Prayers* that had run recently in *Esquire*?

"I would never do that," he said after reading the typescript. "I was trying to show a certain kind of failure."

He also told me that in the years since I'd worked for him, he'd replaced his Rollie with an 8" by 10" box camera which required that after each exposure a cartridge with a new negative needed to be inserted into the camera's magazine in place of the previous one. As a consequence, in contrast to what I'd seen him do, he would now take only a few photographs per sitting.

"I wanted to make it harder for myself, to raise the ante," he said. These days he also wasn't necessarily trying to put his subject at ease: "When Kissinger comes for a sitting, I'm dressed in a suit and tie with my hair combed back; we shake hands, he steps in front of the camera, and I take the picture."

It was a pleasure to be his entourage for several days, with the implicit understanding that he was on vacation and wouldn't be taking pictures. But one evening he said, "You know, I really should get some pictures of the kids. Have you got a camera?"

In fact I didn't, but our neighbor, the poet Bill Berkson, graciously lent us his Leica. The following day Dick had it with him, and I was aware—though just barely aware—that he was taking photographs.

A week or two after he'd returned to New York, he wrote us a letter requesting a recipe for a Sunday brunch dish we'd had at Manka's in Inverness. I duly tracked down the recipe for him, not without a twinge of peevishness—we were exhausted young parents, as I say.

Then we got a package from the studio and discovered that he'd made a book of 35 photographs he'd taken during his visit. Spiral bound, the book was a series of images printed on heavy 11" by 14" photo paper, each sheet glued back-to-back to another sheet with another photograph.

During the period I'd worked in the studio I'd heard whispers here and there in the photography world that without his support staff of assistants and master printers, Dick would be more or less helpless. As we beheld this marvel that rumor died an instant death. Different as it is, in its off-the-cuff fluency this work might even be reckoned a precursor to *In the American West.*

The reader may be thinking a proud father is speaking about a family album of snapshots sent to him by his friend, a famous photographer. The real issue, as I see it, is that Dick himself might have looked at it in that light. When I worked in the studio, he would invite friends and their children up on Saturday mornings to take their portraits—in fact he'd done a session with Lucy and me one Saturday—and then print and sign photographs he chose from the contact sheets and make a gift of them to the family.

There's a loving intimacy in these photographs which, while it isn't a recognized hallmark of the Avedon oeuvre, was nonetheless, as my own relationship with him reflects, very much a part of his nature. It still troubles me that he would adamantly suppress this side of his practice in the work he made public.

4

In May 1981, my father died at 72, having decided not to submit to the procedure for prostate cancer that would have prolonged his life. The following year in August, *Last Rites*, a journal I'd kept during his last days, was published and received a predictably stormy response. There were contending reviews in *The New York Times*—with the *Book Review* weighing in with a rave and the daily *Times* a slam—and there were letters to the *Book Review* in New York, and to the Chronicle's *Book Review* in San Francisco, which also gave the book a rave. In the middle of this for the most part gratifying brouhaha—the letters to me from readers comprising the deepest and most heartening response—Dick called from Idaho, where he was now embarked on his *In the American West* project.

"I was worried by some of the stuff in the beginning, but the end was so beautiful," he said, referring to a healing 11th hour visit I'd made with our younger daughter Cream to my dad's hospital room.

I understood his comment about the first part of the book, where the journal took off in a direction that surprised me as

I wrote it, and amounted to a deferred reckoning with Bill's character that I'd apparently studiously avoided for decades. And I appreciated his being assuaged by the end. For he too was a famous man with a son.

"How are you?" I said.

"I'm fine, except I can't get rid of a headache."

"Maybe you need to rest?"

"Oh, no, the work is going very well."

Andrew Wylie, my agent at the time, had become good friends with Dick's son John and his wife Betty, who had worked for a time in Dick's studio. Striking while the iron was hot with *Last Rites* a subject of controversy, Andrew, an old friend who was just starting as an agent, sold the book idea for *Trio: The Intimate Friendship of Oona Chaplin/Carol Matthau/Gloria Vanderbilt* at lunch one day without a word on paper.

After I received a check for the first third of the advance, the most money in a lump sum I'd seen in my life, Gailyn and I went to New York for a visit, leaving the kids with our Bolinas babysitter.

One weekend morning in Manhattan, we went for breakfast at Dick's apartment over his studio and he showed us some of the enormous "macho" prints from his *In the American West* project, prints made possible before the digital revolution by the 8" by 10" negatives with which he now worked. He set one after another portrait of an unknown man or woman before us, all of us standing as he moved each one in turn to the center of a bare wall where he had them stacked. There was a portrait of a blond waitress who had something of Evelyn's look. Then there was the frightening figure of a drifter who could have been a fire-breathing dragon.

"Who's this?" I said.

Dick shrugged. "Just some guy we met on the side of the highway..."

He obviously wasn't of the Diane Arbus school that befriended a photographic subject, albeit he or she vouchsafed him an immortal image.

"Did you read Sontag's *On Photography*?"

"Of course."

"What did you think?"

I wanted to know especially what he thought of her too schematized commentary on Arbus, who had been a close friend of his.

"Interesting," he said and shrugged.

Before we returned to Bolinas we drove with Andrew out to visit John and Betty Avedon and their very young son at Dick's weekend get-away in Montauk, a place still in the finishing touches stage of construction set on land at the furthest point of the town's coastal promontory. It was another signature of Dick's worldly mastery: a minimalist, light-filled and still mostly empty two-story home that comprised an echoing paradise for all of us on that visit.

Andrew, John and I were the sons of conspicuous "success stories" from the "greatest generation" (Andrew's dad, Craig Wylie, an esteemed Boston book editor), and as our own lives achieved traction were sensitive about this lineage. Betty, the subject of an Avedon portrait then in currency as a postcard, advised John that he was not to read *Last Rites.* And Andrew had told me that Dick regarded me...how shall I put it?... as an unmitigated Avedon acolyte, a description I bristled at, and surely an exaggeration bred of the particular moment the three of us were variously undergoing.

When we arrived and Dick turned out to be there, though leaving momentarily, I was more distant than I'd otherwise have been. That night we watched *Richard Pryor Live* on video and talked into the wee hours. Andrew had recently sold John's book about the Dalai Lama to Knopf. In retrospect it was our own little golden moment.

5

IN 1980, THE BERKELEY ART MUSEUM gave Dick one of his first major retrospectives, and the opening night dinner drew the Bay Area A-List, albeit within certain clearly drawn parameters. Francis Ford Coppola was there, and Bill Graham, and the ubiquitous Herb Caen. Lawrence Ferlinghetti wasn't, nor was Michael McClure or Sam Shepard. When I'd first heard of Dick's *In the American West* project, I'd envisioned him photographing some of these absentees but it turned out to be something else entirely.

It was as if these photographs reversed the circuitry of Avedon's celebrity portraits, taking subjects from the social and economic underside of Reagan-era America, and bestowing *his* fame on them by rendering each in the now iconographic white-backdrop, black-and-white template of the Avedon portrait. While there were only one or two images included in the Berkeley show, these comprised intimations of the masterwork to come.

Carol, Walter, and Lucy had all come up from L.A. for the opening, and Gailyn and I drove in from Bolinas.

"I know I look like a Polish wedding cake," Carol greeted us in her Yves St. Laurent gown.

A day or two later Dick drove out to Bolinas with the Berkeley Museum Director David Ross and his wife, and Marvin Israel, who had helped to design the show. I hadn't seen Marvin since his days at *Seventeen* and during the visit he made an off-hand reference to my early poetry. I looked at him to make sure I'd heard correctly.

"You mean the Random House books?"

He nodded. In 1968 and 1969 Random House had published two volumes of my concrete-minimalist poetry, *Aram Saroyan* and *Pages*, which had received attention as unlikely as Edwin Newman reading each volume from cover-to-cover on the *Six O'Clock NBC News* in New York. Needless to say, these very short poems, including one-word poems, hadn't been unanimously applauded. Part of what surprised me when Marvin, one of Dick's closest friends, mentioned them, was that Dick himself had never said a word to me about them.

Dick asked us to show the Rosses and Marvin the book he'd sent us and then gave me an uncertain look.

"You still have it, right?"

"Of course."

It evidently crossed his mind that we might have sold it in the meantime. We brought it out, and after everyone had turned its pages, David Ross made a remark that may have cut to the quick of Dick's worst misgivings.

"What's next, Dick?" he said breezily. "Weddings and bar mitzvahs?"

I'm trying to suggest Avedon's susceptibility to the cultural gate-keepers despite the protean energy and daring he possessed as an artist. If my minimal poems didn't receive the cultural imprimatur of a good review in the *New York Times*, he wouldn't venture a comment pro or con. If the book he made for us elicited a dismissive remark from an important curator, he would keep those photographs private, and may eventually have destroyed the negatives. If Susan Sontag dismissed photography as a sociologically desensitizing phenomenon he wouldn't venture an argument.*

In late summer of 1984 we moved from Bolinas to Ridgefield, Connecticut, and a year later *Trio* came out. I heard from Carol in the Palisades—where she'd returned with Walter to a much larger house on a wealthier side of town—that she'd gotten nice letters about the book from both Dick and Evelyn, who remained friends though they'd never reconciled. When I ran into Dick one afternoon on Madison Avenue, where he was walking with his studio colleague Doon Arbus, he was cordial but no more than that; we exchanged greetings and went our separate ways.

* As a Jewish Armenian, I'd argue that the advance in the medium between the 1915 genocide of the Armenians by the Ottoman Turks and the Holocaust of World War II ruled out a denial of its crimes by Germany, whereas the Turkish government continues to assert its innocence to this day.

Hosted by John and Betty at their apartment on Broadway and 18th Street, Gailyn and I saw Dick and Evelyn together one afternoon for tea, which turned out to be the last time we saw Dick. After three years, we moved from Ridgefield back to California—first to Thousand Oaks, just north of Los Angeles, and then after the kids grew up, to Santa Monica. Out of the blue, one Friday in February of 1996, I discovered the following voicemail message on our machine:

> *Aram, it's Dick Avedon, this is a bizarre call. Four months ago I reread Last Rites out in Montauk, all alone...a lovely night... in the summer—and tried to call you immediately, and then couldn't find you, and then forgot, and then couldn't find you—tried Connecticut—and then thought what the hell, I'll call Carol.*
>
> *Finally got this phone number. Then, whenever I'm ready to make a phone call, it's dawn in California. So this happens to be an afternoon after an eye operation, so I'm quietly recuperating, and I've been thinking what I've wanted to tell you for so long—that* Last Rites *is one of the great books ever written, I really believe it's literature. I'm a very bad reader, Aram. It takes me so long to get to read anything the right way. But Last Rites was like coming upon some wonderful diamond that had been in the dust. It's thrilling and beautifully written. Never stop, Aram. Bye-bye.*

It couldn't have been very long after that that I sent him a play I'd written loosely based on Lucy and me, Carol and Walter, and asked as a favor if he'd pass it on to his theater pal

Andre Gregory. After months, I got it back in the mail from him, saying cryptically that he was sorry he couldn't help with this. Had he disliked the play? My best guess is that he never read it, and that what he balked at was introducing me into another compartment of his life, as he'd perhaps balked that afternoon on Madison Avenue with Doon Arbus.

When he died of a brain aneurysm during the summer of 2004 at the age of 81 in the midst of preparing another major exhibit, I was surprised, as I imagine many who knew him were, because he was someone you could imagine living on and on. In Paris at the time, I found and saved several front-page obituaries, each with signature images from both his fashion work and his portraiture.

For me, of course, Avedon was a great gift of the years: in his own person, a magician who practiced a kind of human alchemy, quickening the pace of one's life whenever it touched his environs. A friend of his on the East Coast got in touch with Gailyn and me while we were living in Thousand Oaks and asked us to make a video for Dick's 70th birthday.

We asked a friend to film us, and I remember telling Dick as the camera rolled that I'd recently figured out his photographic mojo, based on what had happened to us during his visit to Bolinas. He came into our lives when we were overwhelmed with our duties as young parents, and made us feel privileged and happy and bright and even—after a day or two in his company—freshly energized. Then he took the pictures.

SIXTIES
KID

I GET THAT OUT OF GARDENING

WHEN I WAS IN HIGH SCHOOL at Trinity and during the years I sporadically attended several colleges, I had a number of experiences that I recognize today were as important, as formative, as anything that occurred in the classroom, and probably more so. I came across a book by Alan Watts when I was going to Trinity called *This Is It.* In the title essay, Watts discusses moments, common to people all over the world and throughout recorded time, in which one perceives that one is a part of some larger whole. I found the book tonic for my own development, confirmation of experience I'd known but never discussed or heard discussed. If a man or a woman, you or I, walks outside the house on a particular day and experiences a sense of this oneness, a very reassuring perception in the several instances I recall in my own life, this isn't something that will be the subject of a discussion on *Nightline* or *The Tonight Show.* Nor is it likely to be covered by any print media, not even *The Star* or *The Enquirer.* Watts quotes the following paragraph from *Sketch for a Self-Portrait* by Bernard Berenson, with the prefatory remark that it is "one of the simplest and 'cleanest' accounts of it I have ever seen":

It was a morning in early summer. A silver haze shimmered and trembled over the lime trees. The air was laden with their fragrance. The temperature was like a caress. I remember—I need not recall—that I climbed up a tree stump and felt suddenly immersed in Itness. I did not call it by that name. I had no need for words. It and I were one.

An essentially non-verbal experience of this kind became the subject of one of my first poems, and an ongoing touchstone of my practice as a poet. I'm not sure what year this happened. I still may have been going to Trinity. That seems the most likely scenario because it takes place at the bus stop on the corner of Madison Avenue and 79th Street, where I used to wait in the late afternoon for the crosstown bus to take home to West End Avenue, after an hour or two of after-school revelry at Stark's coffee shop on 78th Street and Madison.

At A Bus Stop

I turned to
an accumulation of women

the instant
a break

the light was so clear
the forms

that instant
exceeded names

outsped
the words

which
follow

follow slowly
like thunder

its lights

Years later I came across a line in Krishnamurti that seemed to refer to this experience: "Between apprehending and naming, is experiencing." If I understand correctly, Krishnamurti says here that in the interval between seeing something and putting a word to it inheres the true experience of what it is, or perhaps more accurately of *what is.* I remember trying to get this into a philosophy paper at NYU, and feeling pretty excited, only to be given an F on the grounds of it having nothing to do with the assignment. This sort of thing frustrated me. At the end of the term, one in which I was enthusiastically engaged in reading Plato and in writing the assigned papers, I received an F. The rest of my courses went no better, and after failing 4 out of 5 of them, with a D in English, an appointment with a staff psychiatrist was scheduled for me.

The psychiatrist turned out to be a dark-suited fellow with dirty fingernails, I noticed. He reviewed my academic record and then looked up at me.

"Well," he said summarily. "There are two possibilities here. One, you're mentally defective. Or two, you have study inhibitions."

"I'll take number two," I said sheepishly. He didn't get the joke.

The philosophy paper may have been read by a student assistant. But the discouragement had the effect of helping to turn me away from the university system, a fateful occurrence in my life. The judgment that my piece had nothing to do with the subject may even have been correct, on balance, because the state I was speaking about is non-verbal, an embodiment of what happens when words disappear for a moment.

Poetry and certain prose works may be the paradoxical effort to portray the state in language. Here is a sentence from Gertrude Stein's *The Autobiography of Alice B. Toklas*, which was written late in her career and became a best seller. In it she adopts the more down-to-earth sensibility of her companion to tell the story of their life together.

The eponymous Miss Toklas is describing an experience of Miss Stein's as a school girl in Oakland (the city about which she famously said, "There's no there there"):

> *She remembers a little school where she and her elder sister stayed and where there was a little girl in the corner of the school yard and the other little girls told her not to go near her, she scratched.*

I'm not sure how it happens, partly at least a consequence of the cumulative effect of the sequence of 38 words before the single punctuation mark, the comma that precedes the two final words—but "she scratched" occurs with a force and presence I find unparalleled. It reminds me of the brief parenthesis in *Lolita* that Tom Stoppard cites, in the profile of the playwright by Kenneth Tynan, as his favorite parenthesis in literature. Nabokov writes:

My very photogenic mother died in a freak accident (picnic, lightning) when I was three.

It occurs to me I'm writing another philosophy paper here, trying to redeem a failing grade of forty years ago. In another experience of my own, I was riding the 79th Street crosstown bus home. It was winter this time, already dark in New York at somewhere between four-thirty and five. I know I was at Trinity because I was worried about homework, lots of it, which I needed to do and hadn't a real will to do nor quite an adequate ability to do. I'm sixteen or seventeen, not a happy camper. I'm twisted with remorse and simultaneously a nervous system unlikely to bend to the required task of the moment, past a certain point. After we'd crossed Central Park, somewhere between Columbus and Amsterdam Avenues, the very stretch it occurs to me now where twenty years later my childhood friend Sandy Kirkland would jump to her death from an apartment building, an estranged wife and mother of two—somewhere in this stretch, it suddenly dawned on me that I was on a bus, that outside the bus, as it moved down the street, it had turned dark, night had come on, lights were on in the buildings that lined the street, and above the buildings was the night sky, and all was right with the world. In that moment, it would seem that my consciousness had switched from its microcosmic state of personal issues and problems, to a macrocosmic awareness that I inhabited a larger universe—that in fact my consciousness was but a single filament of this larger whole.

During the sixties, the poet Gary Snyder, an honorary elder of the hippies of my generation, said: "We must move from a preoccupation with material states to a preoccupation with states of being." Was it a Jungian synchronicity that a chemically synthesized form of this consciousness was widely distributed throughout my generation, like a sort of parting gesture of the industrial epoch itself? In his biography of Allen Ginsberg, Barry Miles records a meeting between Timothy Leary and Ginsberg during the early 1960s in which the two plan for the widespread dissemination of LSD to the new generation to accomplish a revolution in consciousness. I was appalled to read that. During the summer of 1965, when I was 21, and roomed in Woodstock with two actors interning at the Woodstock Summer Theater, there was an evening when one of my roommates, Chris, came back to our place and told us that a waitress at the Espresso Coffee House, the local hangout, had LSD, and it cost $5. Five dollars—at that time a little more than the going-rate for a first run movie. So we had to weigh this—had it been twenty-five dollars it would have been easier to dismiss. Would we ante up $5 to try this new thing? Some people said it produced the equivalent of Buddhist enlightenment, and that the state of mind lasted for eight hours or more. A bargain no less.

I was, then, so I would learn a few decades later from Miles's biography, one of Allen Ginsberg's and Timothy Leary's guinea pigs. Another aspect of this story is that this historic meeting is not discussed. Here were these two leaders of the counter-culture having a meeting and deciding to accomplish a revolution in consciousness. Again there's been no significant coverage. I don't recall even a review of the Ginsberg biography that mentioned this meeting, and yet it seems to me perhaps one of the most historically significant occurrences of the second half of the twentieth century.

What did acid do? It rendered a variation on what I've already described, and quoted from Bernard Berenson, all of which occurred without chemical help. Indeed, I believe that most of us have these experiences but, as they are not the subject of public forums, what is one to *do* with them, finally, except perhaps to forget them?

In the late sixties, just after I'd gotten married, we stayed briefly at The Chelsea Hotel. It was summertime, and one night there was a terrific thunderstorm and I woke up and got out of bed and went over to the window and watched the lightning strike, spreading sudden silent illumination over the city. Then would come the late-breaking thunder, the noise of the lightning, that traveled so much more slowly than the light. I got back into bed and listened to the thunder, entirely unpredictable and yet inarguable, inevitable, and hence as perfect as music—and again there was the sense of being part of something much larger than the self.

When something catches the attention so completely, our thought process gives way to a perceptual level that doesn't involve the mind's insistent duality of good and bad, yes and no. It's snowing! one suddenly sees, and in that moment exists all the wonder of the world without the imposition of any idea of right or wrong, good or bad. T. S. Eliot's famous remark about Henry James, that he had a mind so fine that no idea could violate it, seems to me to reflect such a state as the ideal one for an artist, or perhaps for anyone. Not that James's—or Nabokov's or Gertrude Stein's—characters don't have many and frequent ideas, but that their creator regards them with the same open perceptual gaze and equanimity with which he would notice, say, a blossoming plum tree. The Hindus have a saying: "When the mind empties, the heart fills it."

With that in mind, I want to include one more variation, this one through the auspices of a holy man, Swami Muktananda. Having gone through the sixties and had my moderate share of psychedelic experiences, as well as having had those of the non-chemical kind I've noted, I wasn't particularly interested in the varieties of religious experience that proliferated in Marin County, where we lived with our children throughout the seventies. But one afternoon in 1976, in the Campolindo health food store in Fairfax, I passed a poster of Muktananda I'd seen dozens of times before. It featured a color photograph of the guru, a head shot in which he looked straight at the camera, and as I glanced at it this time—slightly depressed, I should say, as I happened to be that year—I was surprised to see something I'd never noticed before. With a multitude of planets in Leo, I wasn't a natural subject for a guru, but this time I thought I saw in Muktananda's expression not the ego I'd previously assumed, but rather that he seemed to be radiating reverence for the precious passing substance of life, moment by moment.

How nice, I thought, and in that moment my heart experienced a pleasurable melting.

I went home, went to bed that night, and woke up early, as I often did, and lay in our sleeping loft in the dark with my mind going on its usual mental errands. Then I happened to remember the poster and the nice feeling I'd had about it. The poster was a familiar one in Marin County at the time because Muktananda himself was in residence at his Oakland ashram just then. "Be with Baba" were the words that accompanied the photograph, and the details of the Oakland ashram's address and phone were listed. I learned later that around the same time of the morning as I lay awake in the sleeping loft, Muktananda and his devotees were beginning their morning chanting in Oakland.

The instant I remembered the experience I'd had with the photograph—with in fact violent suddenness—the third eye area of my forehead seemed to open and a bolt of radiant energy flooded my body through the third eye aperture. After this forceful entry, I lay, as it seemed to me, bathed in the radiance. This has got to be healthy, I remember thinking. It was like each and every cell of my body was being rinsed in a divine cleansing light. I'll insist that these words, however inadequate, are not a space-cadet's hyperbole but simply the best I can do. Another image that occurred to me was that I felt like a flower on a hillside in sunlight. I had a sense of being alone in the universe and at the same time in a sublime relationship to a providential infinity. I lay in the darkness for an hour or more, I thought, in this state of light and warmth.

When I got up that morning, I went about my tasks but with a sense that I was "looking with the third eye." I'm no longer sure what I meant by that, except that the radiance lingered in everything. When I described to Gailyn what had happened, she told me, "I get that out of gardening." Is it any wonder I'm married to this person?

I called a friend, Tom Veitch, a writer of underground comics, and described what had happened and asked whether he had any information about it. Tom was a sort of Catholic mystic who had spent some time in a monastery in Vermont. He didn't say yes and didn't say no, which wasn't bad as things went, but it was less than I was hoping for in the way of an answer. Eventually I ended up doing some research of my own by reading Muktananda's autobiography, *Play of Consciousness*, which answered virtually all the questions I had.

What had happened to me was called *shaktipat*, the transmission of divine energy from the guru to a subject, and it hinged on an opening in the heart chakra, rather than an intellectual understanding. It could be done by the guru in person and it also could be transmitted through a photograph. What was essential, apparently, was the little melting I'd known in the Campolindo health food store. That had broken me open, as it were, for the *shakti* transmission.

Gailyn was pregnant that spring with Armenak, and as the birth grew nearer, I took up the hindu meditation practice recommended by Muktananda in *Play of Consciousness*. Any man, he says in the book, could make his home a palace of *shakti*, whether he believed or not, by following the simple procedure he lays out. The cover of the book was the same photograph that had catalyzed the *shaktipat* I received.

Muktananda instructed the reader to use the cover photograph as the focus of a regular meditation and the house would fill up with *shakti*. I began to meditate each night and Gailyn told me she felt a palpable energy accumulating in the house. As she grew to term, she herself was as radiant as any guru. And there was also Strawberry, six years old, and Cream, who was three. It was quite a household.

Having thought about Muktananda's precept that *shakti* transmission hinged on an opening in the heart, I eventually replaced his photograph, as the object of my meditation, with Strawberry's first grade school photograph, without any diminution in results as far as I could tell.

* * *

What is one to make of these experiences? What actual relevance to one's life can they have? In the rough and tumble of the years, with their inevitable dark surprises, I sometimes all but forgot about them. When the going gets tough, one would naturally like to be one of the tough who gets going. Only a year or two after the episode with Muktananda, when Armenak was still a baby, I was struggling to get the manuscript of *Genesis Angels* published. Editors and agents were sympathetic or not, but no real connection happened. Meanwhile, all appreciation of ordinary life had gone from me.

My book needed to be published and only *then* would I resume my life. I was a sort of human bullet—and like a bullet, blind, deaf and dumb.

One afternoon after a dentist appointment in Larkspur, I was driving home on the two-lane Olema Bolinas road. It was Memorial Day, Friday. (The universe, I think, can be quite a wit.) I drove up a grade and discovered, at the top of it, that a motorcyclist was coming directly at me—passing a VW van in the oncoming lane—about the length of a car away from me when I first saw him. Oh, I thought, I may be saying goodbye to the world.

The VW van went by in the oncoming lane and I edged my car—a newly-bought yellow Pinto—across that lane to avoid a head-on collision with the motorcyclist coming at me in my lane. The bike glanced off the side of my car, and I braced my left leg against the floorboard—not a good move, I learned a moment later when the front of the car smashed into a grassy embankment beside the road. I knew right away that my left ankle was broken. Though there was no skin puncture, it hung like jelly in my sock. Slowly I began to gather my wits to get out of the car.

I noticed it was a nice day—sunny with a gentle little breeze in the air. Birds were chirping in the bushes close by. And I was breathing in and breathing out, with pleasure in the act itself. For the first time in months, it occurred to me, I was alive in the moment. The moment, likewise, was alive in my consciousness. Apparently I'd almost had to get killed to restore that awareness.

The motorcyclist, a big man who might have been high, was striding up the grade from the side of the road where he'd totaled his bike, shaking his arms at the sky and yelling, "Oh, shit! Oh, shit!"

He came over to where I now lay stretched out on the pavement beside my car. "Are you okay, man?" he said. I told him I was all right.

We both were taken in an ambulance to Kaiser Hospital in San Rafael, and the motorcyclist was released later that day. That night I had surgery for my fractured ankle.

Several days later, I walked in the front door of our house on crutches. The afternoon light in the living room when I came through the door looked beautiful. I lay down on the bed in our back bedroom, physically at a low ebb but feeling glad to be home and mending.

At some point over the next day or two, I remembered the moment, twenty years earlier, when I rode the crosstown bus as night fell in New York, heading home with my heavy homework assignments from Trinity. Sitting up in bed writing a poem about it, I sensed that I was renewing my commitment to a life that had happened in part because of that moment's intimations.

During those first several days at home, I also remembered an agent I'd known years ago in New York, called him, and then sent the manuscript. Within a week after he received it, he sold it.

As the years went by, I began to view the accident as a sort of parable: I'd turned myself into a human bullet in pursuit of my goal. On that Friday afternoon, however, it happened that a motorcyclist I didn't know was playing Russian roulette, passing on a blind hill. As it turned out, I was *his* bullet.

Since the accident, I seem to have a built-in interior warning system that issues an alert when things get so important that they start to preempt the daily gift each of us gets, just breathing in and out. If I go too far afield, I know from experience that that gift could be in jeopardy—and I try to take responsibility and knock off. The moments I've described here seem to have modeled for me in my youth, in an involuntary and heightened form, what today is a more routinely restorative process: one way or another of letting go. For instance, there's a place not too far from where we live in Los

Angeles that serves a nice variation on an English tea, and once or twice a month I'll ask Gailyn if she'd like to drive up there. More often it's time to take a walk.

Paying disinterested attention paradoxically renews the self. There is no arguing, after all, with a fresh morning, a beautiful voice, or a sip of good tea. And the self that registers one or another seems to simultaneously surrender its baggage—ephemeral positions, opinions, attitudes—and, in effect, to grow young again.

THAT'S WHAT HAPPENED TO THE BEATLES

I MET GAILYN AT THE BEGINNING of the Summer of Love, 1967. She was staying over at the house of a friend I had recently made in Brookline, Carol Beckwith. I came across Gailyn one morning in the Beckwith kitchen when I'd come over early to drive down with Carol in her VW to New York, where I was going to meet my editor at Random House, Christopher Cerf, who had just accepted a book of my minimal poetry. Here was this delicate blond woman, with facial features that seemed to cross Geraldine Chaplin and Sandy Dennis, standing in the light-filled kitchen in a sleeveless summer dress, and I immediately felt protective toward her. It was a big dangerous world out there, after all.

Sharing the back seat of the VW Bug on the ride down to New York, we got to know one another. We had similar taste in the visual arts. She also liked the minimal poetry I showed her; I didn't need to explain it since she was familiar with similar work in other art forms, such as Donald Judd's identical metal boxes. I'd never met anyone aside from close colleagues who referred to his work before.

When young heterosexual men live together a certain level of tension and/or boredom seems inevitable because no conversation can be carried into the bedroom. I had been living with other young men for going on a year and I was tired, bored and frustrated. I had a feeling that I was some kind of hard case, that it was difficult for other human beings to understand the way I was.

In the VW, I could see Gailyn's beauty and was struck by our similar taste, but I also felt an undercurrent of sarcasm that surprised me, and which in fact turned out to be an ephemeral thing. It's too bad this girl is so sarcastic, I thought, because otherwise she's perfect. We made a tentative plan to talk while we were both in New York, and I got out of the car on the Upper West Side at the brownstone where I was staying and already knew something was up. I'd been in a kind of despair.

It was important, as I say, that she was so alone, so unencumbered, and of course the fact that she was, or seemed to be, available. These days people will hear that we've been married for more than forty years and be impressed and ask about how we did it.

The most important thing, I think, was that it was possible to do it. I had met exciting women, women who could make my heart or blood race, but that was something else. Gailyn was a lovely woman too, but that was only a part of it. There are lovely women all around, every single day, and not one of them may be possible—for me, nor me for them. With Gailyn, there was a sense of parity.

It's a fateful thing, I think—this extraordinary luck of finding someone who is possible for you, great luck coming forward out of the universe to meet you more than halfway. Today I look back and see where that has happened at critical moments in my life, and I don't know the rhyme or reason for it. Angels appear and things can change for the better. Perhaps what men seek in women, in the end, is less excitement than the solace of a balancing nature, something that allows for a quiet that the spirit of a lone man can't provide.

The actual story of a relationship of any duration is a narrative: this happened and that; this was bad, and needed to be overcome. The first summer Gailyn and I were together, we eventually found an apartment on River Street in Cambridge, a place on the second floor: a floor-through that went from the front of the building to the back of it, and it was there that our life as a couple began. There was now a kind of momentum to my life. After a year in a house on Watson Street, I had a book coming out that I needed to put together.

The apartment was spacious—with a full kitchen and living room as well as a bedroom in between—and we set up my KLH in the living room and played *Sergeant Pepper's Lonely Hearts Club Band* and Vanilla Fudge with these twenty-minute arrangements that were like elaborate chocolate sundaes. I worked on putting the poems together. I didn't want to come across as a novelty, a clever anecdotalist. And yet I wasn't sure what the ordering principle should be. I began to smoke grass again—after a hiatus of almost a year.

With marijuana weighing in and out of things virtually the whole day, I would look out the apartment's side windows toward the Charles River and be vouchsafed various prospects of light at afternoon, evening, dawn and midnight.

Glancing, I would try to savor the life I'd suddenly found: the apartment itself and this person, the very first in my life... and the person who was to endure in my life... whom I didn't feel it a strain to be with. I had been an adolescent of innumerable distant crushes and had needed to pull myself up short or be disabled by so romantic a propensity that I became immobilized.

Poetry in fact had been a kind of strategy to learn how to move—to reanimate after adolescence. But Gailyn has grace that, even in all the years, is still hard to fathom—like a perfect color, or a song you would never grow tired of hearing. Both of us had secretly loved *Silas Marner* when it was assigned in high school. The romance then might be described as both deep and informal. Though I still don't know what she saw in me.

My contemporary Lewis MacAdams and John Wieners, a poet elder, visited one evening—it was now late summer. I was trying to figure out how a book should be put together and it was like solving a problem that had to do with increments of time. A very short poem like:

Pablo
Picasso
and
Casals.

and a one-word poem like:

morni,ng

not only have different durations, they operate on different *principles* of duration. The one-word poem is instantaneous and continuous: like looking out the window. The short poem begins and ends and perhaps repeats.

There wasn't much more I could do with the kind of poetry I'd been writing and I had more or less stopped as I tried to fathom how the poems fit together. The marijuana made it a mental, tunnel-like sort of quest, as I tried to discover a law inside the pieces, a dynamic that would make sense of the whole body of work, and proceeded largely by instinct.

The principle of the book became a gradual move from the short poems to the ones that occurred instantaneously—one or two words—so that there was in fact no reading process. Donald Judd had said that he wanted a work that could be seen all at once and that comment became a guideline for me. The instant poems and the ones that were slightly less than instant were programmatically different. The one-word poem was an image whereas even a very short poem was a guided tour with a beginning, middle and end.

The reader may be wondering how the bills were paid. For the better part of a year, my father had been sending me $200 a month: he had an arrangement whereby he could deduct this amount on his taxes if I wrote him a monthly letter which he designated for tax purposes as a literary resource for his own writing. It was, perhaps, what college might have cost at the time, and I'd dropped out. In those days, an ounce of marijuana cost $15. Gailyn, who could scarcely boil an egg when we met, turned out to have a gift and proclivity for domestic arts and soon we were eating various recipes she would come by and try out.

What a joy to be with her—fresh assurance that things were all right. The work of understanding the poems took up a lot of time, and then on occasion I would see the young man from whom I bought marijuana, whom I'll call Jaimie. He was a few years older than I and could be described as a quick study. A hustler.

Gailyn's parents came for a visit and I can scarcely imagine how I must have appeared to them, suddenly living with their serene and cultivated daughter. I played them "A Day in the Life," the epic final cut on *Sergeant Pepper's Lonely Heart's Club Band*, and portentously announced, "*That's* what happened to The Beatles." It was fall now, and Cambridge began to get dark early in the evening, our big apartment chillier. The tropical, marijuana-riddled summer was giving way to a chill, marijuana-riddled fall. This extraordinary moment, then, is subject to time, to the turn of the seasons.

Marijuana is a whole interesting universe, and as somebody pointed out, best case scenario is to smoke it continuously so that your consciousness is as seamless as possible, given that the consciousness isn't quite your own. It took a little more time for me to recognize the hidden reserves of strength, stamina, proportion, and taste in not being stoned. The benefits of grass, on the other hand, have to do with the vividness of color and sound. And making things slow down so that they can be savored.

One night the phone rang right after we'd made love. It was around midnight, too late for a call even by our sixties' standards. Gailyn picked it up and talked for a while. It was Jaimie. When she hung up, she detailed some discrepancies in things he'd said—about his ex-wife being or not being in town.

"I think he's going to kill us," she said.

Pot paranoia. But all of us were smoking pot and as Delmore Schwartz said paranoids have enemies too. Up to now, I'd been riding the crest of my grandiosity like a surfer who's caught a perfect wave. Now I was teetering.

Space, which is the dimension in which marijuana casts its spell, includes all sorts of stuff, of course, in addition to beauty—things of every variety and shape, not excluding murder. And things had just begun to get good. There were so many doors still to open. In the next day or two my father wired me $1,000—and we fled to Paris with a terrible urgency to avoid death. He knew something was up. And so, having begun with a protective instinct toward Gailyn, I felt a tide of fear and went under—and ran.

THEY'RE *COMMANDERS*, YOU KNOW?

ROBERT DUNCAN, ONE OF THE KEY figures of the San Francisco poetry renaissance of the 1950s in which the Beat Generation surfaced, once said that he didn't believe there was any such thing as a poet. What happened, Duncan said, was that every so often this or that man or woman became, in the process of composing a particular work, *the* poet. And when the work was done, so was the designation. In other words, the poet was a process one entered, not a title—not a noun but a verb. If one were to give Duncan's idea historical application, one might say that whoever became the poet might come to stand for the particular time in which the designation fell to him or her. In the case of Allen Ginsberg, for instance, who first read "Howl" at the Gallery Six in San Francisco in the mid-fifties, the period would date from that reading into the early sixties, when he published "Kaddish," a work of comparable power. Then, according to my personal chronology, a sort of hand-off took place, and the laurel wreath was passed to Bob Dylan, with Ginsberg's personal blessing.

There was Allen, in fact, among those photographed on the back of the first Dylan album I bought, in the spring of 1965, *Bringing It All Back Home*. Up to then, the poets I hung out with in New York—and we considered ourselves the standard bearers in all things—didn't give much weight to Dylan. He was a folkie, and a protest singer into the bargain, and our cadre was decisively apolitical. Joy had nothing to do with politics, and joy was what we were trying to create in our work. In fact, it wasn't a poet who alerted me to Bob Dylan's latest album but an actor friend, who brought it over to another friend's apartment, and when I said something casually disparaging about Dylan, he simply put the record on the turn-table and "Subterranean Homesick Blues" erupted over the room. End of story. There was no mistaking it. It was joy. It was the same joy that was just then beginning to be associated with those two new English rock groups, The Beatles and The Rolling Stones. It was resurgent rock-and-roll, but in Dylan it had found an altogether new, bent, American surrealist, Beat Generation lyricism.

Dylan had gone electric at the Newport Folk Festival and been booed by die-hard folkies to the point of tears, but this new album, including songs that he'd sung at Newport, was, from that first song, the *one* thing he hadn't done before and heretofore evidently couldn't do. It surged through you and made you glad to be alive.

I could scarcely believe my ears. With stoked electric accompaniment behind him, this guy, who a few short months before had sounded like he was trying to impersonate a wise old man—what was *that* about?—suddenly sounded great, young, and *interesting*. It was the spring of 1965 and everything changed. I suppose that's the synergy that Duncan implies with his remark about the poet. "Howl," after all, effectively broke the spell of the consumer-bound fifties. *Bringing It All Back Home* made you feel great—as great as a John Sebastian song for The Lovin' Spoonful like "Do You Believe in Magic?" or "What a Day for a Day Dream" but Dylan was also a broad-based consciousness and that added a heady spike to the mix.

"Bob Dylan's 115th Dream," the epic surrealist vision of Columbus landing in America which closes the album, begins with Dylan starting off minus his band—a musical faux pas—and then erupting in laughter for an infectious long time. Dylan's laugh is deeper than his singing voice, you hear the laugh of a man who knows he's struck gold. "I hate guys like that," my poet friend Tom Clark remarked a year or two later about the newly-arrived Jimi Hendrix. "They're *commanders*, you know?" The same was true of Dylan of course. He had gotten everything right, and there was nothing to do except to listen to it, over and over. That Dylan was serious trouble for any poet didn't change the fact that he was also great, and that comprised a real if not entirely simple pleasure.

At ten, when I lived for a couple of years in Pacific Palisades, my friends had races with the little model cars they sold at hobby shops called Dinky Toys. One of us sat in the middle and raced all of the cars, one belonging to each of us in a group of four or five, around and around a circular track determined by whatever reach one's outstretched arm commanded. Whoever sat in the middle could have cheated at will and made his own car, or the car of his favorite pal of the moment, the winner. But we were kids and our egos were easily subsumed by the visceral drama of the race itself. We trusted the ring master to lose his head and simply bring in the winner who was slated to win that race. Amazingly enough, I don't remember any arguments about who won. Artists' egos, perhaps, have to be a little like that.

It was right around here, too, that the paradigm shifted decisively to rock as the vehicle for the *news* for our generation. As the sixties went into gear—and 1965 seems more or less the start-up of that epoch—few of us took a daily paper, because it was understood that you weren't going to read the truth there. We knew, for instance, that there was something dreadfully wrong with a headline like "13,000 Advisors Sent to Vietnam." Still, *The New York Times* printed it with its implacable straight face.

There was a lot of anger on both sides of what was deemed "the generation gap," and Dylan is a great poet of anger. If the hippies were largely a middle class phenomenon, their fathers and mothers were understandably upset that little Johnny and Betsy had grown up to be such shits that they didn't give a damn about what Mom and Dad struggled so hard to achieve. Johnny and Betsy, on the other hand, were listening to the music, and the music said don't wait, we want the world and we want it now. Dylan told us, in a tight arrangement with Al Kooper's heat-grill of an organ vamping behind him.

He went on a creative roll over the next couple of years, following *Bringing It All Back Home* with *Highway 61 Revisited*, and then the double album *Blonde on Blonde*, which served notice, if any further notice was needed, that he was a creative phenomenon who left everybody shifting in his wake. It was during this period that The Beatles hit their stride as art song writers with "Penny Lane," "Paperback Writer," and "Strawberry Fields," and The Rolling Stones loosened the blues to include lyric lines that wouldn't have been likely a year or two earlier from the Lords of Muddy Waters: "Jumpin Jack Flash," *et al.* It was the psychedelic sixties by now, and it was Dylan, I think, who found the fullest verbal equivalent to the retinal and aural circus. And Dylan, it should be noted, was said to favor amphetamines. I once ingested some methedrine with the idea of noticing its impact on composition, and Dylan's work of this period might be seen as an unparalleled exemplification of that chemical venue. What can happen is a kind of sustained double entendre (a pun allows you to hear two voices at the same time, both William Empson and Robert Duncan instructed): *Blonde on Blonde* as a title was simultaneously a lament on his romantic life and an off-the-cuff echo of the Russian suprematist painter Malevitch's high modernist "White on White" in the Museum of Modern Art. Dylan was planting a nicely contoured boot in every camp imaginable—from Jasper Johns to Eric Burdon, from Charles Olson to Albert Einstein. And when he hit top-forty radio with a song reputedly about Edie Sedgwick called "Like a Rolling Stone," it was hard for anyone not to hear him. I was in Woodstock that summer of 1965 and glimpsed Dylan a number of times at the Espresso Coffee House, one night in heated though not audible vituperation with Sally Grossman, whom I knew slightly, his agent Albert Grossman's wife and the woman featured with him in the cover photograph of *Bringing It All Back*

Home. (Someone once told me that the woman in the cover photograph, whom I knew to be Sally, was actually Dylan in drag—the equivalent of the de riguer rumor when a new male artist became famous that he was gay.) That summer I must have listened to "Like a Rolling Stone" dozens of times with delight on the radio and on the jukebox at the Espresso without deciphering any of the lyrics but the tidal wave of the chorus: *How does it feel?* By the mysterious synergy that allows an artist to speak for a particular moment, one might venture that there was a multitude of answers to the question posed: as many answers as there were *of us* on the verge of launching this voyage that became the sixties, one that would take many of us a long way from home. There was a deep emotional throb of goodbye in the chorus, and also an empowering melodic rush in it. It would be years before I read the lyric sheet and discovered the character portrait Dylan had conjured of a young Sedgwick-like figure at large in the world without Mommy, Daddy, or checking account. In these new songs by Dylan, there was the same coruscating wit that wouldn't hesitate to shoot a fool down, but there was also a new emotional empathy coming into play in "Like a Rolling Stone," and in the song that took up the whole of side four in *Blonde on Blonde,* which was said to be about Dylan's wife, Sara, "Sad-Eyed Lady of the Lowlands."

One had a sense, too, of an artist having accomplished in a few short years what many might not realize in a lifetime. The largesse of the double album was even a bit wearying, at least to this admirer, although one played it as compulsively as one had ever played an album. The repeated saturation in the music is one element of the sixties culture that has all but eluded comment. When *Blonde on Blonde* came out, it became for a good many of us the new soundtrack of our lives. It was as if Dylan on the turn-table all day and night in the households of his peers, was laying in a template of sensibility that would follow us into our future lives, like a B.A. or a law degree. It was, perhaps, what Fitzgerald meant for his readers in the twenties, and what my father had meant for them in the thirties. A far closer interface was possible, however, in the era of electric media. Dylan having made top-forty radio now had unprecedented reach in our newly christened global village. He was The Poet, and also, as in any such apotheosis, a great deal more than that. He became for several years—outstripping The Beatles and The Rolling Stones, groups after all, for all their individual genius—the living model of what we were and/or what we aspired to be.

There is, of course, a lot of pressure in being that—in trying to be that as a parent, for instance, let alone as a role model for a generation of one's peers. After the release of *Blonde on Blonde*, Dylan dropped out of sight, and there were rumors, though not confirmed in the media, of a serious motorcycle accident, one in which he had barely avoided death, and for a stretch of over a year he was out of the picture. And that was the year the sixties went right over the falls.

I had met Gailyn just after the release of the Beatles album *Sergeant Pepper's Lonely Heart's Club Band.* The song "Lucy In the Sky with Diamonds" was said to be a transcription of the acronym LSD. As a couple we had baptized ourselves in the psychoactive sacraments, so to speak, and then smoked ourselves under the table. As winter rolled around, the Great Paranoia descended and we fled to Paris. After a Franco-American comedy of errors trying to get my father's Opera district flat installed with central heating, we fled Paris for New York. I was scared. Years later when I alluded to the fear I felt, which belied marijuana's reputation as a benign recreational drug, Jim Carroll remarked that he thought one crossed a point of innocence with a drug, after which the drug knew you as well as or better than you knew yourself, and things could get crazy, whatever the drug might be. Being with Gailyn, having a book of poetry coming out with Random House, and smoking marijuana to stay relaxed—I was walking the winter streets of New York with the sensation that buildings might fall on me. As this happened, The Beatles and The Rolling Stones both came out with albums positively rancid with psychedelia, as it occasionally struck me despite the fact that I was a self-annointed true believer: *Magical Mystery Tour* and *His Satanic Majesty's Request.*

Then Bob Dylan came out with an album that was like a pin prick to the whole lopsided circus balloon. It featured a cover with a black and white photograph of Dylan, with short hair, in a buckskin jacket standing somewhere in the country with several people one didn't know. The album was *John Wesley Harding* and featured a stripped-down acoustic sound and a different voice than one had heard from Dylan before, full of plaintive resonance, singing Bible-like parables out of the Old West.

Dylan simultaneously made his first concert appearance in more than a year with Pete Seeger and Arlo Guthrie at Town Hall, and it was like his return to the family fold, the folk roots that had once nourished him, now a man who had walked through the fire. It was a heartening spectacle just then. It was as if he'd called us up from wonderland and delivered us back to the side of the lake.

As a couple, Gailyn and I were now on the mend, having stopped smoking grass and each of us attending sessions with a psychiatrist in which we learned that invaluable lesson for any couple, how to have a fair fight. By February or March, my fear had receded. Walking home from my appointment with the psychiatrist one afternoon, as I rounded the block where we had a studio apartment, East 81st Street between First Avenue and York, a bum sitting with his companion against the side of the building in the sunshine, looked up at me, still long-haired, and said, "Good afternoon, father."

"Good afternoon, son," I said, eliciting the bum's ragged laughter and my own surprise.

The next Dylan album, *Nashville Skyline*, with a new countryfied Dylan singing "Lay Lady Lay" and doing a duet with Johnny Cash, seemed to shore up the back-to-basics line of *John Wesley Harding*. Dylan was now a family man, and I had a brief encounter with him in Woodstock during the spring of 1969 right after the album appeared. I was just married and Gailyn and I were on the macrobiotic diet and deep into the hippie fashion palette of the day. Dylan was driving his children around in a wood-paneled ranch wagon, the modestly attired country husband and father. When I told him, sitting in the driver's seat of his wagon, how much I liked *Nashville Skyline* he looked pleased and even a little surprised. His voice and presence, both on and off the album, seemed that of a man far older than his twenty-eight years. And well it might. While he would go on to create many memorable and beautiful works, his moment of apotheosis was just then turning—he had shepherded us through a dazzling, perilous decade, even while the news of the demise of other key figures had begun to arrive. Dylan was the preeminent artist of the sixties, our Shakespeare, and his survival into the present seems not the smallest of his many miracles. But then, his predecessor and friend and supporter from the outset, Allen Ginsberg, had also survived his turn as the Poet.

Privileged kid iwth dad, 1946.

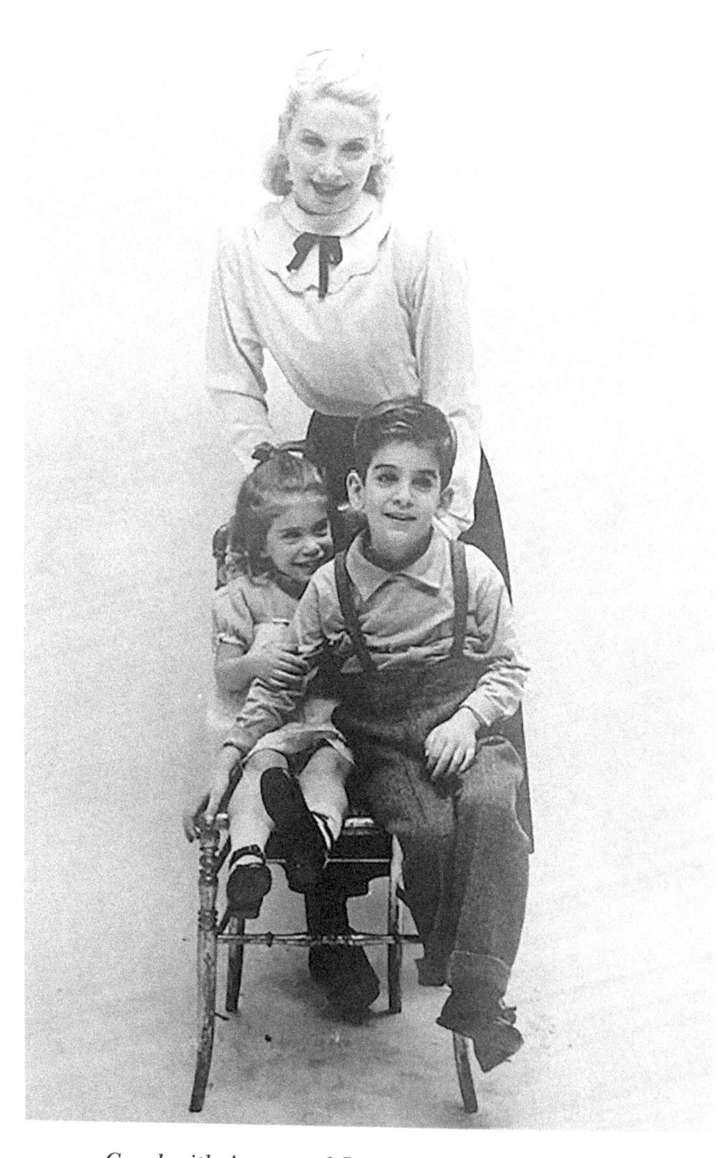

Carol with Aram and Lucy, New York City, 1949.
(Photograph by Milton Greene)

William Saroyan and older brother Henry after the death of their father, Armenak, Fresno, 1911.

Mom Carol as a foster child, 1927. Bill was touched by the way her finger and her thumb were touching. William told Aram, "I fell in love with your mother's past."

Bill in London, 1944, with Ross Bagdasarian (r), co-creator of the song "Come On-A My House" and the enduring novelty group, The Chipmunks.

Portrait of handsome man about town;
William Saroyan in his prime.

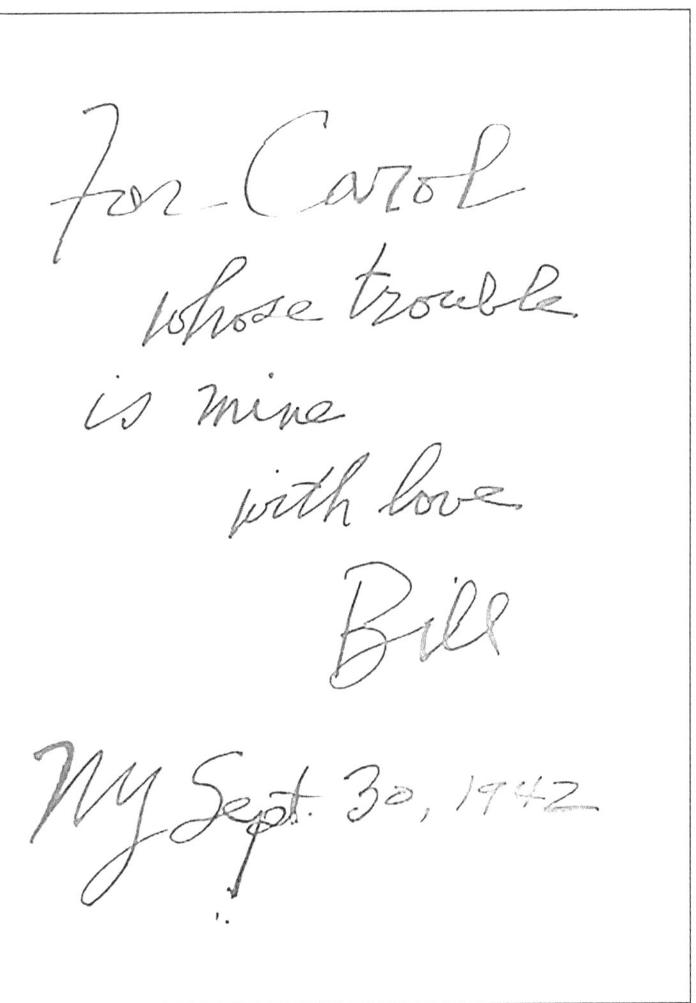

For Carol
whose trouble
is mine
with love
Bill

NY Sept. 30, 1942

This is Bill's inscription to Carol in his book of stories, The Trouble with Tigers.

Martha Stevenson, Sam Marx, Bill and Carol in Hollywood, c. 1947.

Carol and Aram in San Francisco, 1947.

Self-portrait by William Saroyan, Friday, August 30, 1963, a day before his 55th birthday, San Francisco.

NOVELLA ONE:
DESTINY

SIXTY

In his sixtieth year the world had been taken over by jackals, so it seemed to Philip Klein. Each day one was given incremental reports of an endless war dance, featuring as heads of state people one would have avoided in high school. The visages, his own age or older, appeared to be *boys'* faces, aged without the mediating touches that lend a face its adult signature. Something gleeful, teasing, or, alternately, threatening played out in the eyes and mouths of these figures in front-page photographs. Klein could only riffle through the morning *Times*—the society, including the newspaper itself, seemed to have a reverse magnetic force, as if it were jettisoning him.

On Tuesday morning, before getting out of bed, he falls back into a dream state, or perhaps an actual dream, and finds an idea long simmering in a bold new realization. Later that morning he calls Jason Rider, a rock star since the sixties and now an activist.

"If a bunch of us chip in, say, $100 each, we could buy a billboard and put 'War Is Obsolete' up on it."

"Right on," Jason says. "I think it costs about $2,000 for a billboard so we'd need about twenty of us. That's possible. I'm just not sure people will get it."

* * *

THAT MORNING HE GOES TO A rehearsal of one of his plays at The Actors Studio. The director is a Persian woman of indeterminate age—maybe older than Klein—with a far wider culture than is customary among the run of theater people he knows, but a hesitant, faltering command of English. After discussing his two-character romantic comedy over the phone, she has cast the roles with two outstanding players within the Studio's parochial pantheon.

Theater in Los Angeles, he understands, is made up of these separate cells, little enclaves that bolster and buoy their members. If you're not 24 and a star, acting is no walk in the park. The actor who plays the man is a studious Stanislavskian and, it develops, much too fiery for the more contemplative half of the couple.

"What does this line mean?"

"I don't know, beyond the obvious."

"That doesn't help me as an actor."

The female actor is temperamentally a better match for the male role and allows the other actor to preempt the rehearsal process with microscopic textual bone-picking.

Several years earlier, in the first flush of a burst of playwriting he never imagined, he raced around town setting up one-night-only staged readings at various venues—Beyond Baroque, The Stella Adler, Venture West and First Stage. On the night of his first play reading, at Beyond Baroque, it was as if he was turned inside out—then after a heady half-hour of greetings and congratulations in the lobby, it was time to go home.

* * *

Klein dreams George W. Bush apologizes to the nation on television, speaking from the Rose Garden at the White House.

"My fellow Americans," he says standing at a microphone without his usual entourage and appearing drained and chastened, "I've betrayed you. I've betrayed myself, my wife Laura, my daughters, but worst of all, I've betrayed you, the decent, honorable citizens of our great country."

Because of what we've been through, he muses as he sits on stage, Jews hold onto power tenaciously. On his right side, sit the two heads of the Actors Studio's Playwright/Directors Unit, Mark Schaefer and Harold Idel, and, to his left, his director, Rafae Yarra, a small woman trembling.

He's withdrawn his play from the reading of it scheduled for tonight because the male actor hasn't improved but in the meantime the other role is now ideally cast, which makes the performance worse. With both actors cast against type, there was still the possibility of chemistry. With both actors fiery, the lines don't play at all. Instead of a duet it's one note all the way.

He tries to explain this in the meeting at the Greenwood Theater on Fairfax. "To withdraw your play like this," Idell says, "is, in my opinion, reprehensible. It's an outrageous disregard of the work of these actors. I can barely understand a human being who could be so callous of his fellow artists..."

He's "on," all faces turned to him.

"I understand you feeling that way," he says looking at Idell, a famous director now perhaps 70, and gets to his feet. "And I respect it. And I think, under the circumstances, I shouldn't be here." He begins to walk to the edge of the stage to make his departure.

"Aw, come on, Phil," Schaefer, a thin saturnine man with dark circles under his eyes, says behind him. "Don't leave. Look, we've got to discuss this..."

Actors, directors and, last and least, playwrights. These two were sincere, honorable oldsters, most likely needing a venue to dispense their wisdom and nurture while he has his graduate writing class. And Rafae, on the other hand, was an Iranian refugee seeking a cultured society in which to flourish, or at least a modicum of solace and shelter. Alas, the Studio is mostly made up of Jews.

In the lobby, the bluff, brash, gangster-like Ron Warsh comments, "They're a different *culture*. They *fuck* differently."

Didn't everybody he wonders, his own love life virtually subterranean. Sheila no longer reaches for him and he can't bear a skirmish with a negative outcome.

"The theater in L.A...." he essays.

"Oh, come on..." somebody in the audience calls out.

The hunting and gathering he practiced has undergone a qualitative change. The big drive that subsumed him sexually, an urgency that had found in Sheila a beautiful if not always compliant partner, has waned and he stands before his class at USC imparting his wisdom like an alternate form of self-perpetuation. And when a hiatus occurs, summer or the winter or spring break, he misses the weekly appointment.

Meanwhile Sheila has joined a group involved with the historic preservation of their development, Village Green, which now has National Landmark status—the two of them moving outward in lieu of the erstwhile drive focused on one another, home, hearth, children.

"There he is again," she says, glancing out their living room window at the vista of greensward and half-century old trees.

"Who?"

"Eddie." A longtime resident now subject to an influx of new residents interested in historic landscape preservation.

He glances out the window. A large figure who seemed to be jobless, Eddie stands beneath an enormous sycamore holding a clipboard.

"What's he doing?"

"Good question."

"It's like he's making a house call."

"He's planting trees that have no place in the historic landscape."

"I'll go get my gun."

"It's not funny."

"Bush has the character of what he is," Sheila says Saturday morning before getting out of bed. "He's a dry drunk. He stopped drinking but never went into recovery. So he's impatient, into instant gratification, loves attention..."

She leaves early to attend the march against the war in downtown Los Angeles. He leaves later in the day to give a free writing workshop at the Brentwood Library, a recruitment tool for a private workshop.

He recognizes Michael Shane amid the crowd at the opening of the Wayne Thiebaud retrospective at the Frederick Weisman Museum at Pepperdine in Malibu. It's nice to recognize someone at a significant cultural event. Usually there is a curious absence of familiar faces, as if he and Sheila travel in the wrong circles. A husky fortyish native of Bakersfield, a painter married to an actress, they have a little boy. He's fresh from New Year's in New York.

"It had just snowed. So quiet—beautiful."

Thiebaud, the painter of cakes and pies in the first wave of Pop Art, Klein discovered as a Manhattan high school boy. Could such paintings endure? As well as Monet's haystacks—the end of a stick of butter in one gleaming like a transcendent moment of an ordinary day.

"I saw Earl," Michael says. "Ran into him at the Brice Marden show at Matthew Marks. He's old and cranky these days."

"How so?"

"He's telling me he hates all the painters of the eighties—Schnabel, Salle, Fischl. They've ruined painting. Jesus."

"I thought he'd moved back here again."

"He has, he was there scouting for his gallery."

He dreams Sheila betrays him with a young conductor of chorale music in Los Angeles. He glimpsed them together in a garden setting where she took his arm and they walked with a brisk commanding stride, Sheila beautiful and youthful.

He wakes less stung than he would have been a decade ago. It wasn't that he loved her less but knowing his own mortal limit. No one can take away the beauty of his life with Sheila, even if she left him.

The Actors Studio has expelled him after he withdrew his play a second time. Rafae and the others were gone from his life.

Later that afternoon in the garage, he dislodges a box of copies of an old novel, the box a lower one in a stack. He'll sell the book that evening at a writing workshop at the Beverly Hills Library. A heavy swivel chair stacked upside down on top of a file cabinet comes loose and brains him on the side of his head. The chair now lies on the garage's cement floor. He's okay, his senses intact, but doesn't know the damage is minor.

In youth, a blow was a blow. Now it takes time to realize the extent of the damage, the body is slower even in pain. He rearranges the stack of boxes, replaces the chair on top of the file cabinet, and puts the box of copies into the trunk of their navy Volvo.

Driving with Sheila, they listen to Bush's State of the Union message but arrive at the library before it ends. Later that night the highlights on the news feature the President crisply mispronouncing the word "nuclear," a smiling Laura Bush clapping—her arms extending outward at her elbows and then coming together with a slow, steady pace, as if she's keeping time at a square dance.

The next day in the mail comes the announcement of a concurrent New York show of six enormous aerial landscapes by Thiebaud. There's an iridescence to the painting on the card: A river surrounded by farm land, roads, trees in the surrounding landscape in late afternoon or early morning sunlight. Such enormous paintings are athletic feats, homages—as if he's bidding the planet a fond aerial goodbye.

CARAPACE

KLEIN DREAMED OF A 70S TV star, Jimmie Walker, a tall skinny African American with a pronounced Adam's apple and a deep voice that had a rasp to it. His signature exclamation, enduring beyond any memory Klein had of his actual persona in the show, was the word "dynamite" rendered with singular, much-imitated relish "*Dy-no*-MITE!" In the dream, Jimmie Walker had fashioned a tiny puppet out of his own fingers—the fingers creating the movement of the mouth of this tiny being.

He realized it was a dream about his son, Luther, whom he hadn't heard from in a while and no longer knew how to contact. It was the little face made up of Jimmie Walker's fingers that was his son.

As a boy he'd been high-strung, energetic, blond like Sheila—the sunshine of their lives, with some inestimable tension between father and son: Klein the thinker, the muller, and Luther, the doer, a boy in love with real space, air, playing, fun, all day long—until exhausted, carried in Philip's arms and laid down in his bed asleep.

They didn't talk to each other, Luther seeming to speak a different language, at once urgent and fearful, and Philip thinking you'll be fine. And Luther better than fine—at baseball better than he'd been. He coached a Little League team to get him to play and then he proved to be a central, pivotal player—one of three that put the team in contention.

With any addict, you hit a wall. He had to go back to Little League, almost twenty years ago on the East Coast, to recover the devil-and-angel that graced their lives.

"So how are you?" he said on the phone.

"I'm in my car right now. I'll have to phone you back."

"Okay."

He didn't call back and both his cellular and pager numbers were disconnected when he tried to reach him again.

On a pleasant Saturday afternoon in April, walking on Robertson to a gallery opening, Philip and Sheila encountered a squat smiling Indian man in a three-piece suit coming the other way who gestured to them warmly.

"You are very lucky man, sir," he told Klein, his index finger touching the area of his third eye. "He is very lucky man," he said to Sheila, who wanted, Philip knew, to move on immediately.

In the commotion that ensued the man gave him a little crumpled-up ball of paper, asked him how old he was and what his favorite number from one to ten was, and wrote his answers down in a small loose-leaf notebook. He also asked him what he did and when he answered that he was a teacher and a writer, told him he was going to be very famous. Then he asked if he still had the crumpled-up piece of paper.

"Yes."

"Let me see it," the man said and when he opened his hand, he picked up the crumpled piece of paper and then put it back down in his hand and asked him to open it. When he did, he found the two numbers he had told the man—61, his age, and 8, his favorite number.

"I am a Yogi," he said. "You will be very famous. You give me forty dollars now for this."

He gave him one of two twenty dollar bills he found in his wallet and went on to the gallery. The exhibit was the work of an artist born in 1900 who had died in the early sixties. How did the Indian man get the two numbers right? And what exactly would he become famous for at this late date? Giving $20 to a charlatan?

He woke at his usual four A. M. and said his prayers. It was a warm night and before long it would be summer again.

When he talked to Luther, he wasn't talking to his son, he was talking to a drug or to alcohol—what Luther was currently addicted to, who knew. And when he reached out to him, it was as if he touched hard carapace not tender flesh.

The Indian crumpled the piece of paper into a little ball, then asked if he still had it; and when he said he did, said, "Let me see it." When he opened his hand, he took the little ball of crumpled paper and then gave it back to him and asked him to open it. Ah. He'd replaced it with the piece of paper on which he'd written the correct numbers, which he'd crumpled up in the meantime. Why crumple up the paper that way? A crumpled-up ball of paper would be easy to replace with a second crumpled-up ball. In the early morning, the mind was clear and a small riddle like that could be solved.

HOUSE EXCHANGE

In the late summer of 1966, the summer of mod and rocker London, when John Lennon met Yoko Ono at the show of her work in the gallery at the Indica Book Shop, Klein stayed with his father, Otto Klein, in a one-bedroom apartment at Whitelands House just off the Kings Road in Chelsea. The old man was in his late fifties, had won and lost several fortunes in American real estate, and was "doing some loafing," he'd told Philip when he phoned from New York about the advisability of a summer visit with him.

"Of course you can come," he said. "I'd enjoy seeing you, but I want to warn you I'm not hep or hip or whatever you say these days. Go about your business as you see fit. I won't advise you. I have no advice in this social revolution."

"That sounds wonderful, Pop."

"Well, good, my boy. When will you arrive?"

Almost four decades later at the beginning of a seven-week house exchange Sheila arranged for them in London, they sat together on the 24 bus as they passed a block of Council Housing flats.

"When I did that—"

"—the world would have managed, somehow," she said, beside him in the front seat on the top of the double-decker.

The Council flats reminded him of meeting a young English poet, Stephen Leigh, and his blond wife that long-ago summer. He and his poet friend Tom Wright from Chicago had paid a visit to the two one evening.

Stephen Leigh's wife was beautiful. They had a little baby. They were obviously poor, and the marriage wouldn't survive much longer. Leigh had already written and published a poem celebrating his affair with Henry Bailey, a New York poet about twice his age.

It was an apartment painted pristine white, barely furnished, with literary items brought to the table with two hands: special limited editions, rice paper folios, the printed word like a minted coin.

"I wonder what happened to Stephen Leigh's wife," Klein said that evening walking near their apartment in Covent Garden.

"Who?" Sheila said.

"Or Steven himself."

"Shall we go to the Crypt at St. Martin-in-the-Fields?"

The evening of his arrival his father had allowed him to smoke marijuana in the living room of their flat, where he'd sleep on a sofa. Otto nursed a little glass of brandy while he rolled and lit up a joint.

"Go ahead," Otto said. "Each man has his poisons."

And what had his been? Boredom, perhaps, and an inability to put up with an intimate relationship. Yet by the time of the London visit he seemed cherubically at home in himself.

"I want to give you some very ordinary, non-controversial advice," he said, immediately reversing his scenario. "I hope this can be non-controversial. I don't know what's going on, but try to see this in the clear light of day.

"You see, real estate works differently than the stock market or any other investment. Say you put $10,000 down on a property—a ten percent down payment..."

Would he be able to understand what his father was going to tell him. He'd scored his grass at Indica, and it had already proven surprisingly good.

"What's the matter?"

"Nothing, why?" He looked at his father and at the cloudy English early evening out the big bay windows.

"Oh, you're stoned, I hope it doesn't affect your brain. You've got a good brain, you know. Not a fast one, like mine, but a perfectly good one..."

"Thanks, Pop. Go on—I'm fine."

He and Sheila settled into their seats at a table at the Crypt in the basement at Saint-Martin-in-the-Fields church in Trafalgar Square. Sheila brought a piece of apple cake with clotted cream with two forks. He'd gotten two glasses of water.

Otto died without liquid assets, and although he had properties these were inside a conglomerate that made any legacy to Klein a thin one. But his real estate advice that afternoon had at last been heeded.

"I can't figure out why my parents hate me," she said and looked away.

Her parents were being evasive regarding their Notting Hill flat.

Sheila arranged their house exchange sensing this legacy wasn't hers. "The World War II generation thinks the sun rises and sets on their lives," Philip said, "—which now that I'm old, I know is crazy. These secular humanists don't get it..."

"Sixty is the new fifty," she said smiling.

"We can't use the place anyway," he said. "They're both going to live to be a hundred. They don't hate you, it's me."

That evening's program at St. Martin-in-the-Fields was Bach, played by the church's chamber ensemble. Sitting in an upper stall, he listened as the music filled the space in a celestial evocation of—youth, he couldn't help feeling. He remembered her as the girl just out of college—the delicate buoyancy and beauty of her stride. It was a sentimental thing to be a human being, Otto had said in passing that long ago summer.

After the concert the streets were packed with the overflowing conviviality of the pubs.

"This is wonderful," Klein said on the second floor of Kettle's Yard, the house in Cambridge that had been turned into a museum after the death of its owners. The three-story house was filled with minimalist paintings, sculpture, and pottery, as well as smooth stones gathered and arranged by color on a wood table—dark yielding to lighter grays—along with bird feathers, small pieces of driftwood, and other objects of found art.

It was Sunday and they'd taken the train from London to Cambridge on an impulse. The rain fell heavily for a few minutes while they sat in the living room with its Brancusi bird among other pieces.

When the downpour let up they walked into the center of town and shared a piece of cake and a cup of tea at EAT. He thought he glimpsed Tom Raworth, another poet from that sixties summer, wheeling a baby carriage, the passenger probably a grandchild, in front of the shop's picture window. Their eyes didn't meet and most likely it wasn't Tom Raworth—but even if it had been, it wasn't likely he would have recognized Philip if they'd locked eyes.

2

THE DREAM COMMINGLING OF KLEIN AND Martha Stewart wasn't entirely without rhyme or reason. They were probably not that far apart in age.

Then in the dream's finale, having performed in a vague sexual tableau—he'd touched her naked back lightly—he was rejected by Stewart on the basis of his inferior standing in the larger community.

Otherwise things were good. He and Sheila had made love again after long abstinence. And he'd discovered a reservoir of love he harbored for his long-dead father.

Waking up in Paris, in a package deal Sheila arranged at the Hotel Malte Opera by the Palais Royale, it occurred to him that the dream might have to do with Sheila's mother,

Charlotte McBean (nee Shwarzer), to whom he'd recently written on Sheila's behalf.

"We need to move on, as you've so brilliantly already done," he said at breakfast in the hotel dining room.

"I think I may have dreamed about Charlotte," he mentioned an hour later, walking through the 360-degree vistas of the Tuileries gardens.

"You think—what does that mean?"

"It was Martha Stewart, and I was humiliated."

"You're ruining this."

"It was a dream."

"She's nothing like Martha Stewart."

They walked over the crushed granite and sat down on a wood bench, looking out at the gardens.

"Now that I've seen this, I think I understand how the French would—or could—"

"Did she say anything?"

"Martha Stewart?"

"Yes."

"Not really."

At the top of the Champs-Élysées, they went into the American Drugstore and got a table in the café.

"There was no give in the letter. She's still complaining that you got married and had a life."

"Perry at Village Green designed this," Sheila said, indicating the interior of the restaurant. She looked out from her seat against the wall while he sat facing her. He turned around to get the general palette of the place, grays and browns, muted and soothing, like their Uruguayan neighbor.

Among several phone calls he made from the hotel, only Jay Fielding, a poet he'd last seen decades ago, proved reachable. When they got out at the Père Lachaise metro station, he wasn't sure how they'd recognize him, but within seconds he knew it was him crossing toward them, a rugged middle-weight who'd let himself go a bit.

Planning a tour of Père Lachaise, Fielding suggested lunch first and had them settled at an outdoor café within minutes. He gave news of others in the expat community, and several times referred matter-of-factly to an imminent break-up with his French partner, the mother of their seven-year-old son. He also spoke of Jim Brodey, a poet their age who had died of AIDS a decade ago in San Francisco. During his last months, in steep decline, he'd told nonstop stories of Frank O'Hara, Auden et al, that he wished he'd taped.

"He was a liar and a thief, but somehow you wanted to hear him."

Wandering Père Lachaise after lunch, they paused at Oscar Wilde's extravagant tomb with an Epstein Greek-style sculpture commissioned by a devotee.

"It's sufficient," Fielding said, nodding at the monument.

"His life's coming apart," Sheila said that evening. "He was very gracious, considering."

The following day, exploring the Marais district, they discovered a geography of asides: serendipitous squares, gardens and courtyards, in which often there was very little going on other than light, shadow, stone, and silence. And maybe a cat.

"French women wear these tops you can see their bras through," Sheila said at tea at a café in a tiny square catty-corner with the Picasso Museum.

"We're in Paris," she said, her eyes twinkling.

3

HE PUT HIS BOOK DOWN ON the rug under the living room sofa. It was an afternoon in the second phase of their sojourn, staying at the second of their two house exchanges, a ground floor flat on South Hill Park Road in Hampstead, the back of it overlooking the pond with swans in it. Sheila was up the hill at Fenton House, taking in the garden.

The next afternoon, after sharing a lunch plate at Kenwood House at the top of the Heath, the two explored the paintings.

"You need to walk into the corner over there and see the Vermeer."

He went over to it and took in the signature light on the forehead of a young Dutch girl playing a guitar in the seventeenth century.

The two met with her parents, Edward and Charlotte, one afternoon at Burgh House, near the Hampstead tube stop, and walked with them slowly toward their new exchange address. Sheila had prepared a tea, and purchased at a Hampstead deli a cannelloni entrée for dinner.

Charlotte, in her eighties, paused at the top of Willow Road and looked back at a Georgian house on the higher corner.

"This is where our friends the Nestors lived for many years. He was the number two man at the British embassy during the Suez crisis and was knighted—darling, when was Harry knighted?"

Edward McBean, a retired American diplomat several years older than his wife, had a prodigious memory, the repository not only of the family's history, but much of the world's.

He paused to recall the date. Whenever Charlotte mentioned someone there was usually an introductory threshold to be negotiated in which that person's lineage and bona fides were lightly reviewed. He'd grown fond of her because beyond the obsession with bona fides, he'd discovered a lady who viewed the world with a dismay usually immediately overtaken by curiosity.

"1964," Edward offered.

"Yes," she said, turning to Philip, "he had the perfect death. Would you like to hear how he died?"

"Yes."

"His wife Lotte was out shopping and was caught in a London rush hour. She phoned Harry, who had stayed home, and told him that he should pour himself his before-dinner drink, and simply turn the oven to 350 to heat up their lasagna, which was already in the oven—and she'd be home in time to take it out and serve it. When she got home, Harry was in his favorite chair with his drink, and the lasagna was ready to serve. But then she discovered that Harry was dead.

"Wasn't that the perfect death?"

The dinner went smoothly with no mention of the Notting Hill flat.

While both McBeans had slowed down noticeably, they were still getting around and after dinner the two couples walked downhill to the bus stop onto the 24 bus.

"Good job," Philip said after they'd seen the two of them.

"Let's walk home inside the Heath," Sheila said, taking the lead, walking away quickly. "It's not uphill."

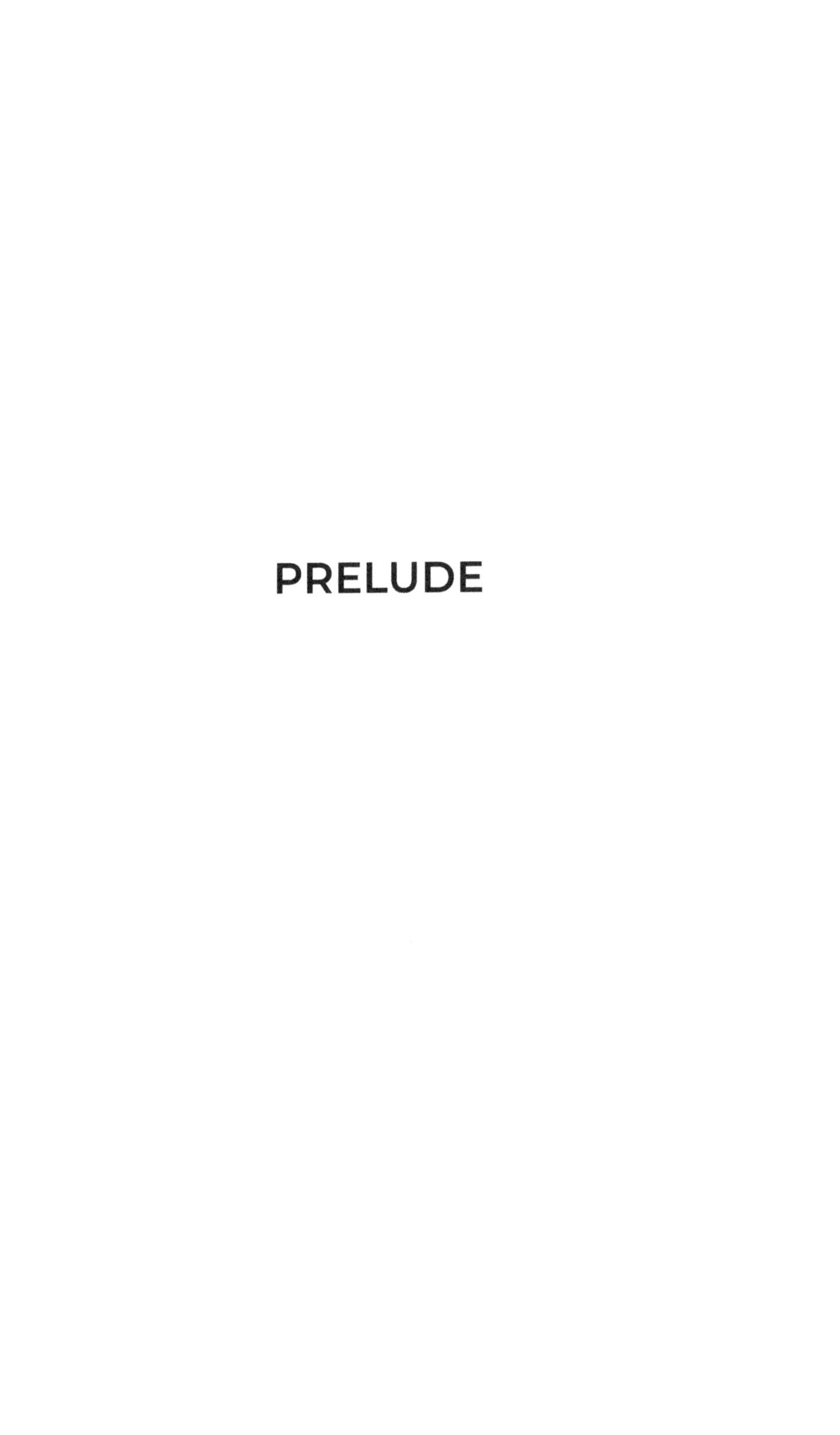

PRELUDE

BEVERLY HILLS IN THE FIFTIES

WHILE MY MOTHER SLEPT ON A foldout couch in the living room, Lucy and I shared the bedroom. She and I had twin beds on either side of a night-table. In the room's darkness before we fell asleep I instituted a program called "Assembly," modeled after school assemblies. I introduced talent, frequently a singer, and then went on to sing a song ("Sixteen Tons" maybe, or maybe "Mr. Sandman"). Most likely I was trying to restore order to our shattered reality, and remember feeling contentment as I went about this semi-nightly ritual. Lucy was ambivalent about it—sometimes protesting that she wanted to sleep, sometimes joining in with a song or an announcement herself.

In the early fall of 1951, we'd moved with our mother from a small mansion with an orange-tiled roof on North Rodeo Drive to this one-bedroom apartment in a four-story apartment building on the corner of Olympic Boulevard and McCarty Drive. My father and mother were getting divorced for the second time, their second marriage having lasted six months. I was almost eight years old, Lucy five, and my mother just twenty-seven.

It happens that our stay in that apartment corresponds to the dawning of continuous memory in my life. Before it I see scattered glimpses: an apartment with gray walls near the Plaza Hotel in New York where my parents broke up for the first time...the bridal path down the center of North Rodeo Drive where one quiet sunny afternoon I taught myself how to ride my bike no-handed...But from the apartment building on, a narrative coalesces.

Martha Stevenson is a friend of my mother's. A pretty young Southern woman, a blond with delicate, finely chiseled features, she was married to the band leader Hal Kemp who died in an automobile accident after they had been together only a few years. Their daughter, Townsend, is a year or two older than I, excellent in school, and a know-it-all. One day at Martha's Beverly Hills house, Townsend asks if I can do a swan dive.

"Yes," I say.

"Really?" She's genuinely impressed. "Can you do any other dives?"

"A jack-knife."

"A jack-knife? Really? Can you do a flip?"

"I can even do a double-flip."

A week or two later I'm poolside with Townsend. She awaits my swan dive, jack-knife, and double flip. I go to the diving board, walk to the end of it and, after a brief hesitation, dive.

"Why did you *lie*?" Townsend asks indignantly as I get out of the water.

But for some reason Townsend's mother, Martha, takes an interest in me, and probably I owe my passage through this crossroads of my life to the kindness of this gentle woman. She has a slightly sidewise smile—a trait I recognized years later with an immediate sense of trust when I met Gailyn. Martha arranges for me to be baptized Episcopalian, and I am, and then promptly enrolled at the local Catholic school for the third grade.

My reading is poor, and it isn't helped by the introduction of the Catechism, of which I understand barely a word. Often I'm ordered to stay in the classroom during recess, kneel at my desk and recite 50 Hail Mary's in repentance for my poor performance during class. My mind seems to be a repository of tension, electrical static, which limits my capacity to learn. However, when I get on my knees in the empty classroom and let the words of the Hail Mary go through my head, although I don't understand them, I find myself actually praying.

On regular evenings during the school year Martha takes me to the minor league baseball games that take place in Los Angeles. There are two local teams, the Hollywood Stars and the Los Angeles Angels, and they play each other over and over again.

The fresh green and white of the unused baseball diamond at night under the stadium lights thrills me, and the brightness of the players' fresh uniforms as they take the field at the beginning of each game. Martha has season tickets, a box between home plate and first base, and she patiently teaches me how to keep a box score. At the start of each game we settle into our seats with the programs and the little sharpened pencils that come with them. At the end of the game we've each neatly filled in our play-by-play record. As we leave, Martha tosses her program into the trash, but I hold onto mine, though I never go over one again. But it's evidence that I can still learn how to do something correctly, which is important to me.

What the psychological mechanisms are, I'm still not clear about, but one afternoon when I kneel down on the sidewalk in front of our apartment building and hold up the front end of my bike in order to spin the front wheel—as the wheel spins in front of my eyes, I experience a hypnagogic hallucination. All of the noises of the neighborhood, as well as my inner monologue, turn into demonized gibberish. It's as if all noise becomes sonically wrinkled, and this pattern of wrinkles threatens to take over my mind so I won't understand what I'm hearing or thinking. I have more than one of these episodes, but none so severe or long-lived that I can't hold on to my identity through it. None lasts more than ten minutes or so.

I also sometimes experience noises made by Lucy in the apartment as if she's making them entirely for the purpose of annoying me. If she's in the bath, for instance, and I hear her splashing in the water as I lie on my bed, the splashes take on a quality of smug contentment that I hate.

"Stop making that noise!" I shout at her from the bed.

Hannah, a German émigré painter and another of my mother's friends, does portraits of Lucy and me, both in the German expressionist manner with bold strokes of primary colors.

Hannah's boyfriend, a tall easygoing American named Ted, is the first person I meet who is said to be a poet.

Michael's a—*green* name," he says to me one evening in Hannah's living room in West Hollywood after we've watched a game show based on charades.

"Green?" I say, uncertain what he means.

"Don't you think it's sort of a green name—Michael?" he asks, very relaxed and off-hand.

"I guess so," I answer, warming a little because of his manner.

"What color would you say the name Sam is?" he asks.

Instantly a color leaps to mind. "Black?"

"Good!" he says. "You got it."

Eisenhower is running against Stevenson for the first time, and Beverly Hills is full of red, white and blue *I Like Ike* buttons. There are fewer *All the Way with Adlai* buttons.

One late afternoon as I ride my bike around the neighborhood, I encounter a boy with a great mop of curly dark hair also riding a bike. We seem to strike an instant rapport and ride around on our bikes together for a while. His name is Josh. When it's almost time to head home, he asks which candidate my parents want to win.

"Stevenson," I tell him.

"Mine too!" he answers, delighted.

As if this parallel ratifies our natural rapport, we both immediately stop our bikes, get off and embrace each other.

Around the corner from our building is a little cobblestone alley. My friend Tommy and I like to play and explore there in the warm sunshine after school and on weekends.

Just off the alley, an old man has a workshop with pin-ups on the wall.

There's the famous one of Marilyn Monroe stretched out naked across red velvet, and one of another voluptuous blond with her breasts visible in a white fur coat.

One afternoon, in our wandering up and down the alley, we find a small bullet in the crevice between two cobblestones.

"Don't touch it!" I shout, holding Tommy back.

"Why not?"

"Fingerprints," I remind him.

"Oh, yeah. I'll go get something to pick it up with. You guard it."

He lives in the corner house on the alley: a normal boy with a normal family who all eat Rice Krispies for breakfast. He returns in a moment with a paper napkin.

Carefully, we pick up the bullet with the napkin, and then walk with it to the police station.

"Can I help you boys?" the officer behind the counter asks.

"We'd like to report a bullet," I say.

We open the napkin on the counter and the officer looks at the bullet.

He asks and we tell him how and where we found it. He takes this information in, thanks us, and keeps the bullet. Leaving the building, I feel a little surge of pride for having done my civic duty. It's late afternoon now. As we walk down the steps, Tommy pokes me.

"Look," he says. "It's Red Skelton."

Dressed in a white suit, the red-haired comedian is coming up the steps we're walking down, and we turn to watch him.

At the building's landing, he approaches a group of blue-uniformed policemen standing to one side of the doorway.

"Break it up, boys," he says, "or I'll call the cops!"

As a part of the divorce agreement, that fall my mother, Lucy, and I move into a brand new ranch house in a development in Pacific Palisades. As the Eisenhower era goes into gear, our life settles down for several years into a tranquil (and for my mother deadly boring) suburban routine: the car pool, public school, neighborhood friendships, and, for me, the Little League. I forget about going crazy. I want to hit a home run.

YOUNG LOVE

SHE WAS A FRIEND OF MY mother's, and my first memory of her is in a horse-drawn carriage being driven down a sunny street in Geneva, Switzerland, toward my aunt Elinor's house. I'm ten years old. My mother has brought Lucy and me from California to Europe for the summer, and somehow this woman, the English film star Kay Kendall, is in the carriage with us. It's love at first sight.

Let me describe her skin. It's tan and absolutely smooth. Her face and in fact her whole body has an elongated nobility, a fashion model's cool perfection. Then there's her voice. It's somewhat throaty, with an English accent that is somehow calming—but it's not the voice, exactly, either. What it is, is this combination of the physical and vocal—the body and voice of a goddess—with the spirit and the fast impulsive wit of a comedienne. She is telling us, all of us, in a spirit of democracy that would never jostle the features of a goddess of *Vogue*, about how much she hates her boyfriend, with whom she's just split up.

"He's horrible, darling, what can I say?"

My mother laughs. And I, emboldened by her charm and openness, tell her I think her ring, a platinum band, is beautiful.

"Oh, darling," she says, addressing me directly in the dappled sunlight passing over us as we're driven along the tree-lined avenue, "you must have it."

"*Absolutely not*," my mother insists loudly.

The actress, who has now removed the ring from her finger, stands up, wobbling precariously in the carriage. I never saw her drink very much and yet she had this perennial air of tipsiness. Stunningly beautiful, she had the vulnerability of the congenitally absent-minded. She made me at ten feel protective of her.

"I'll throw it away, darling." She makes a gesture of tossing it overboard. "I swear it. Unless you let him have it. I *want* him to have it."

"But darling, he'll lose it," my mother answers.

"I don't care, darling. I don't want it. I'd forgotten I was wearing it. It's from that human horror."

And so the ring was given to me. Too big for any of my fingers, nevertheless like a wedding ring it sealed a vow of love in me as deep as it was instantaneous.

A day or two later, as my mother had predicted, the ring was gone. I remember going to sleep with it under my pillow, and in the morning it wasn't there. I have no idea how it was actually lost. We were in Switzerland, I couldn't speak French, and I didn't have my own room. I searched for it for a day with Lucy, sensing my crisis, helping. At twilight, I searched the foundation of a house being built in a grassy field between my aunt's house and the house of her nearest neighbor. Lucy tried to offer her comfort.

For me the gift of the ring was, I think, simply the currency between us, arrived at spontaneously, improvised by Kay without being aware of my feelings, which in fact the gift helped to precipitate. The word got back to her—I'd been crying and that must have been some kind of giveaway. She never let on.

As our summer in Europe continued, she took a trip with my mother, Lucy, and me, and I got to know her better. Beneath her charm and antic quality, she had a melancholy side that touched me and made my insides swim as if I'd had some sweet wine.

On a train ride through the Italian countryside on our way to Portofino, she told me she had no sense of taste or smell. I remember wishing, with the passion of an impossible disembodied love, that I could disappear into her beauty and give her my senses.

I never saw her again, after that summer. My mother brought Lucy and me back to California and then moved us all to New York where I continued my life into the turmoil of adolescence and the dark, awakening secret of sex. My own first love had already occurred, an exotic bloom unqualified by the limits of what is possible between two people. It was pure ideal, as the memory of a departed parent one never really knew might be. And some years later, Kay Kendall, in her early thirties, died of a blood disease. By then I knew who she was, I'd seen *Les Girls*.

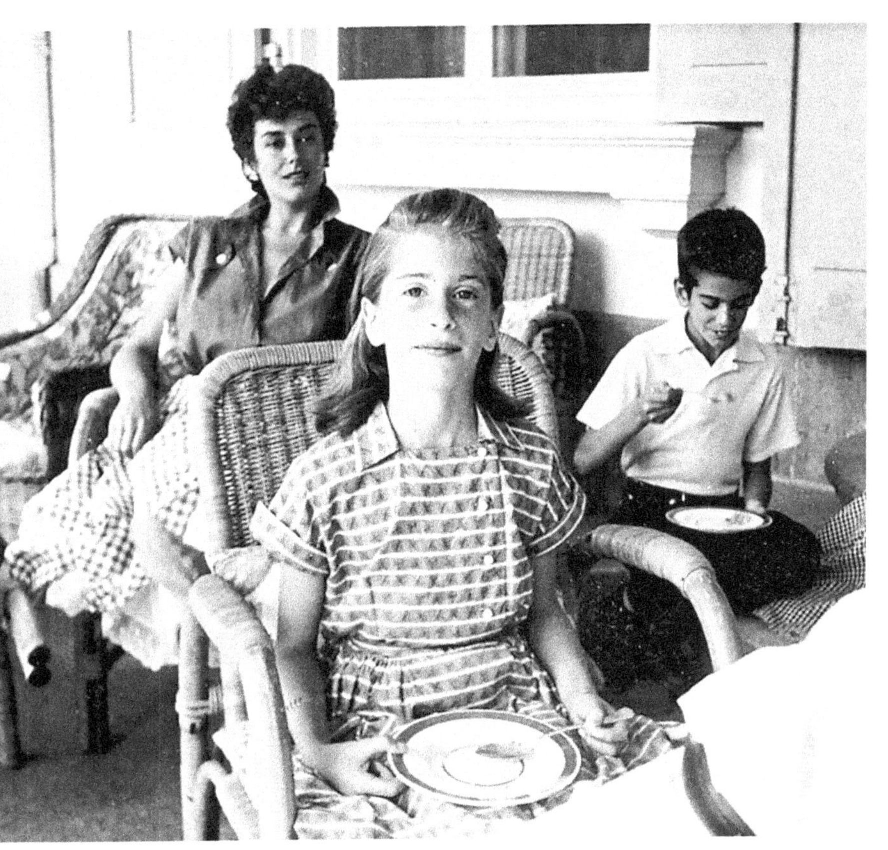

Geneva, 1954: (l. to r.) Kay Kendall, Lucy, Aram.

Signs of the times.

Carol and Walter, Los Angeles, 1961.
(Photograph by Aram Saroyan)

Drawing by Aram Saroyan.

Headshot of Lucy Saroyan.

On the set of "Kotch," Los Angeles, 1970. Walter (holding unidentified child actor), Charlie, Gailyn (holding Strawberry), and Aram.

Booksigning for The Romantic *at Dutton's Brentwood, 1988.*
From left: Aram, Gailyn, Walter, and Jack Lemmon.
Photograph by Harut Sassounian.

The most expensive word in history.

William Saroyan, 1959.

Aram at Crystal Cove, north of Laguna Beach, California. (Photograph by Vincent Katz, 2023)

NOVELLA TWO:
OUR ROMANCE

MY HOLLYWOOD

1

I VISIT MY MOTHER IN HER upstairs cocoon of a room in the big house in Pacific Palisades and wear a mask of amiable equanimity.

"How are you, Mom," I say, leaning over her bed to give her a peck on the cheek. She sits on the bed Indian-style in her floral robe and pajamas.

"Oh, all right," she says and lets out a sound that's half a sigh and half a giggle. "Your old Mom's just okay—not great." She shrugs and I see she's hovering close to tears.

"Joey's not doing well?" I ask. Joey had retired, I should say, because he was so ill with narcolepsy that he fell asleep on the phone with some of his agency's biggest clients.

"Your weekend grosses were…terr…—*Zzzz…*"

And Clint, or Sly, or whoever it is, is wondering if that's "terrific" or "terrible."

"He's all right, darling…But it's a day-to-day thing."

He was once found at the corner of their street, holding their little poodle, Mayo, by a leash—asleep on his feet.

My situation is that I now have a gig selling Mazdas in Oxnard, but this isn't the same universe that these people inhabit. My mother enjoys the idea that she was never married to my father, Rex Elson, who played first base for the old Triple-A-League Hollywood Stars when I was a baby, and stole 26 bases one year. The fact that his TV career never really took off after *El Paso* was cancelled after a couple of seasons didn't really make a difference financially. Rex lives comfortably on his real estate holdings with his second wife down in Palm Desert and plays golf 50 hours a week. That Mom attracted Joey Wando, and eventually divorced Rex and married Joey, is the biggest feather in her cap, and she'd probably prefer not to be known about at all before she married Joey, the head of International Famous.

I always used to wonder about that. Did somebody not go to school?

But the client list is amazing and, to be honest, these are charming, accomplished people with, of course, huge bank accounts.

I get a five thousand dollar bonus for moving ten Mazdas in a month and I have to compare it to what Joey or one of his clients makes. It's like an hour's work for them, maybe two or three hours.

"The only money I have that I ever thought was my own…"—my mother is saying. It's half a mill she has stashed somewhere and imagines will perk my curiosity. It might, if I thought she was going to give it to me. I'd send it to my ex-, Susie, so she could quit her job. I'd take our son, Todd, to Europe.

It's twilight and the sprinklers just went on outside on the lawn one story down.

"Darling," she says, "if you could do anything in the world, anything at all, what would it be? Whatever it is, no matter what, just say it."

What does she think I want to do? This is another game, though, and I shuffle through some options: Buy a nice townhome on the Oxnard beach. Visit Venice (Italy).

"I'm happy," I tell her.

"You're the best of us all," she says. "Will you stay for dinner, darling?"

I'm here because she invited me for dinner. I ponder whether or not she actually forgot or this is some kind of power move.

"I'd love to," I tell her.

2

THE PERSON WHO TOOK CARE OF me when I was a child wasn't my mother, but a wonderful, soft and serene African-American woman around my mother's age, a Father Divine disciple he had christened Morning Light Ray.

For a Black woman of the generation that came of age at the end of World War II, maybe hitching up with a white princess was a smart thing to do. In any case, there Ray was, living with us and being a soft round mountain for me to climb on and hold onto.

Her face had such imperturbable beauty.

Fifty years later, her pension fund somehow disappeared.

Once, when I was a child, I went to one of her meetings with her. I remember the delicious creamed corn they served, and the heat in the huge room, filled with banquet tables, the multitude of bodies and voices—the warmth of those lives. She was one of their successes. She had taken their message of love into a family of wealthy American white people.

I met a man who had grown up for several years with Ray taking care of him and his sister during the period when my mother had to let her go, between her divorce from my dad and her marriage to Joey. He came into the Mazda dealership, and although he didn't end up buying, we discovered this coincidence in our lives. After Ariel married Joey, she asked Ray to come back, and Ray left this man's family to go back to work for her. We talked for a while and when he expressed great interest in seeing Ray again, I let him know how to get in touch with her.

By the time I spoke to Ray several weeks later, he had made contact and met with her. The way he'd spoken to me, it didn't seem a remote possibility that he would invite Ray to live in his home as an honored guest with his wife and family. She was that precious to him. I asked Ray how things had gone when they met.

"I think he was a bit awed, dear," she said.

"By what?"

"Well, you know, I think he was a bit awed by the house."

She was saying the man was awed by the big house in the Palisades. Ariel had been treating Ray badly for years, and it had come out now that her pension fund had been pilfered. It was as if she was getting off on the appearance of things, rather than the reality she knew first hand.

As Joey lay dying, Ariel went a little nuts, firing and rehiring Ray several times, selling off properties, writing people in and out of the will, and making overtures toward a new life for herself in New York, the city of her dreams when she was young and beautiful.

Here was Ray, in her seventies, having given her life to us, laid it down with love, and she didn't have anything to show for it. An island of serenity when these people were in their power-charged primes, now as an old woman she would elect to throw herself on Ariel's mercy, which the rest of us knew was a bad idea.

Ariel's low blood pressure and personality need a pageant to keep her pulse quickened. And she enjoyed the movie stars who were Joey's clients, and letting someone else have it—*POW!*—to keep things moving. She and Joey had grown distant as time went by. She couldn't remain beautiful forever, even with body wraps, face lifts, collagen, Botox, and the rest.

The irony is that both Ray and Ariel, ebony and ivory, were virtually immobilized in their seventies by arthritis. I would see Ray in the kitchen at night as I was leaving after I'd been over for dinner in my mother's bedroom. While my mother was set up on her bed upstairs, where she'd been all day with her phone and her TV remote, Ray would be hunched over the butcher block center-piece in the kitchen, still on her feet, but laying all the weight she could on the counter top.

Now she wore a different look than the one I'd known as a child. The beautiful unruffled countenance had been replaced by a kind of bemused doggedness. It was as if she was saying, I'm here because it's my life, and I don't have anywhere else to go.

"Goodbye, dear," she'd say softly as I leaned over to kiss her goodnight on the cheek.

Then I'd step out the back door by the electronic gate, and walk out to the sidewalk and my car, breathing the good air that blew up from the ocean around there.

OUR ROMANCE

HE'D BEEN AT HIS DESK ONE afternoon in the showroom when the call came.

"Jerry?" a woman's voice said.

"Yes," he said. There was a yellow Miata five feet from his desk, like a work of art.

"It's Lacy," she said, and gave a quick little laugh.

A cousin in her late thirties, his mother's sister's daughter, living in a small town in rural Pennsylvania with her husband and daughter, "How are you?"

"I'm okay, but I think Sally may be about to check out."

"Oh?"

"I really do."

He'd talked with her a month ago, and then phoned Sally in San Francisco, and ended up talking to her in the hospital, where she'd been admitted after a fight with her boyfriend, who'd broken her jaw. He was in his twenties and he'd never spoken to him.

That night after making himself and Todd cheeseburgers and salad, he went into his bedroom to phone her while Todd watched *ET* in the living room.

She answered the phone, but early in the conversation handed him off to her boyfriend. She had to go somewhere.

"Hey, Jerry," said the boyfriend.

"How are you?" He didn't know why he should be talking to this man who had so harmed his sister.

He sounded young and—unlike Sally, who always had a kind of Broadway edge—stoned.

"So, you know," he was saying, "that was when I'd been doing that. I will never, ever, harm your sister, again, man—ever. I love Sally more than I ever loved any person in my life."

When he saw her for the first time in San Francisco as she stepped into the living room of their hotel suite, it was as if all the bets of their lifetime were off. She had done such violence to herself that he couldn't question her authenticity, as he'd done for decades. Her whole body was riddled with sores and abscesses and she must have weighed around eighty pounds. She was close to death, and still there was a bravura in it—it was another signature gesture. Yet her face had the gravitas of a death mask.

"Hi, Jerr..." she said with a little smile.

"Hey, Sal..." he said.

Brian, a professional who was choreographing the intervention, invited her to sit down in the living room.

In another period of their lives, she'd lived for over a year in a SRO hotel in Manhattan, and when Ariel offered to buy her an apartment, she refused.

Another time she'd torn up a $10,000 check, a "Christmas bonus," in Ariel's face. This was the signature of her life—these extravagant, death-defying leaps in the face of poverty and the abyss, and their mother.

At the Stanford Court in San Francisco, they sat in the nicely-appointed living room. She was an addict who was nearly fifty years old and she either had to stop or she would die. An old maid living in her late paternal aunt's house in the Sunset District while the estate went through probate, she made the place a neighborhood crash pad, allowing young runaways and addicts to crash there.

This wasn't covered in the Great American Songbook, which he'd sung and played with his trio until the bottom fell out. Rodgers and Hart, Frank Loesser, and George and Ira Gershwin hadn't touched it. He'd officially signed off for a day, Friday, and come up on a Thursday, his usual day off. Saturday and Sunday were big days on the lot in Oxnard. All sorts of people came in about Mazdas.

It was getting toward dinner time and Brian was going to order room service. They couldn't take Sally downstairs to the dining room. He didn't know what to say to her and she was uncharacteristically quiet. She needed several thousand dollars to pay her dealer. It was a routine addict maneuver, Brian had coached him and Lacy, who had flown in from Pennsylvania. It was Ariel who had chosen the Stanford Court. Nothing but the best for my little girl. There, a song: *Nothing but the best for my little girl.*

Lacy shared a room with twin beds with Sally. She had to agree to the intervention; there was no legal means to force her since she was over twenty-one.

Lying in the queen-size bed that night in a bedroom at the other end of the suite, he realized Northern California, where he'd lived for a decade and where his father had grown up, had never quite done it for him, though the Jerry Elson Trio had once had a regular tour of the environs—Jack's in Mill Valley, Yoshi's in Oakland, and Downstairs at the Fairmont on Nob Hill.

One afternoon years ago when he was still married, driving over the mountain from Stinson Beach into Fairfax, where he had a gig that night, he'd found Johnny Mathis on the dial singing "Stardust," which at that moment seemed to distill his parents broken romance from beginning to end: Rex Elson, the baseball player, and Ariel Light, as his mother called herself for a couple of years when she had little parts in movies—two young and handsome people without much of a clue, other than this exact music, which could be misleading.

Sally's boyfriend, David, was at large in the second floor two-room California Street apartment the next morning, a sleepy, slightly rotund young man to whom he nodded as they entered. Sally had preceded them and arranged for the payoff with the dealer. Now he saw memorabilia of his sister's life, photos of her as a sleek siren of the sixties from *Vogue*—the power agent Joey Wando's step-daughter, headed straight for—for hell, it turned out. Dating this, that and the other king of the industry. The fact that she would eventually find David and settle into serious addiction seemed to him maybe the exact turn that he'd registered as she entered the hotel room. Late in the day and lethal as it was, she'd transcended the gaga swirl of their heritage. David wasn't famous, rich or above average otherwise, it didn't seem, and yet she'd cohabited with him longer than with any person in her life.

Brian managed to take her with him on a flight that afternoon to Philadelphia, where he ran a rehab program. David was given several hundred dollars to go away. Maybe Sally had enough in her to last through the flight.

On Saturday morning, he was back at his desk in front of the yellow metal masterstroke of contemporary design. An affordable sports car so small that you might even imagine for a moment that you could lift it. In fact he'd tried it, one afternoon when nobody had been in the showroom, and couldn't.

THEN AND NOW

ON A CLEAR SPRING DAY, ELSON got a telephone call at work from an old girl friend, someone he hadn't seen for thirty years. She had spoken to his friend from Pacific Palisades High School, Steve Steinberg, who relayed the fact that he was divorced and told her how he could be reached.

"I just decided to call. I know it's probably not the right thing to do...,"—words he couldn't quite get the gist of, sitting at his desk in the show room.

"It's not wrong," he said, watching Ruben Pacheco smiling at a tall smartly-dressed young woman looking at a black Miata in the corner of the showroom. He figured Ruben was getting close to a sale when he began laughing with her.

"Well, Jerry," the voice on the phone said and then paused as if he was supposed to take the ball from there.

Her name was Nancy Spears and he remembered her vividly because their connection was innocent, but intensely, and more or less exclusively, sexual.He remembered her as small, dark and shapely, with an expression that seemed to harbor blood imperatives. As he was leaving a party one night, now a college drop-out, she said to him: "I'm just your little mule..."

What did *that* mean?, he wondered that night as he drove around in a boat-like Chevy Bel Air that belonged to his mother and step-father's cook. He'd hardly spoken to her in high school, although he'd often noticed her.

It meant, he found out a night or two later, that the two of them were like pieces of a sexual puzzle that happened to fit together. She was even more beautiful with her clothes off and he merely had to hint at something to see it happen.

"It's great to hear from you," he said. "Where are you?"

She lived in a high-rise apartment building on Ocean Avenue in Santa Monica. She'd gotten divorced several years ago and had no children. She still had her looks or, more accurately, was recognizably the same person, now in her fifties—which made them, he supposed, more or less even.

She invited him back to the apartment after a dinner that cost more than he could strictly speaking afford at Shutters-on-the-Beach—but it seemed to be pay back time: the woman had put up with a lot of post-adolescent nonsense from him when he imagined he was a combination of Frank Sinatra and Jackie Wilson.

"Where are your CDs?" he said upon arriving in her eleventh floor apartment. There was a large picture window that held a view of the dark beach with the lights of the Santa Monica pier at the far end. He'd known that view from the back of his parents' cars from early childhood, driving home in the dark from outings and parties.

"In the corner," she said from behind the counter divider that marked the kitchen. "You see the Bose there? It's got a CD."

He made a beeline for it. It was an uneasy moment, their arrival in these private environs, and he could tie up his mind and at the same time contribute something to the next segment of the evening.

The place was done in a sort of beach style, the furniture mostly white with pastel bolster pillows.

"A little cognac?" she said.

"Great," he said. He had picked out a CD of Nat King Cole and George Shearing and in a moment "September Song" started up.

"Oh, nice," she said, coming out with two little glasses. He stood up and took one from her, then sat down on the sofa. She sat poised forward in an Eames chair opposite him.

"I love him," he said. "Every note he sings is music."

"If I had a piano, I'd ask you to play and sing," she said.

"Oh, no," he said. Occasionally he would sit down at a friend's piano and vamp into the past.

Easier in conversation than he remembered, she seemed in full possession of herself, whereas what had been surprising and sexy about her in their youth was that she seemed half-possessed by powers beyond her conscious reckoning. Only her laugh, which was deep and full of body resonance, brought back the young woman he remembered.

The loosening hold of his own sexuality, what he liked about his fifties, was also what worried him about it. Viewed in a positive light, it seemed to infuse all of the visible world with a gentle gleam of eros. In a less positive light, he seemed to be losing the vital charge of his life.

Men his age were taken with twenty-something women because they were like Energizer Bunny batteries—new life for the old bones. Yet he looked with sadness at the idea that he would corral such youth for his own purposes—not that there were any available candidates.

With Nancy Spears, at least for this moment, it was like the best of both worlds—one of those Cracker Jack plastic cylinders that displayed a different scene when you tipped it in the light.

"I remember you," she said. "You were attractive..."

"Thank you a lot."

"I didn't mean it that way," she said smiling. "It was just that you didn't seem to think much of anything else, and even being the little lemming that I was, it still worried me."

He laughed out loud. "Oh, come on," he said. "You were as bad as I was."

"I don't want to make love, if that's what you're thinking," Nancy said.

The album had ended a while ago and they were sitting together on the sofa looking out into the darkness of the night sky above the ocean. The lights of a passing plane twinkled across the black vista.

Some sort of obligatory move was probably on the agenda, but the inertia he felt obliterated whatever it might have been and instead he was enjoying their quiet companionship. "Okay," he said.

"You're different," she said. "Was your wife mean to you?"
"Not at all," he said. "What made you think that?"

"So in other words, we're just enjoying things."

"Yes," he said. He turned and after a moment of eye contact kissed her. "That's nice," she said and drew him back into the kiss and inserted the tip of her tongue into his mouth.

"I'm going to go now," he said without moving. After a moment, he stood up.

"Can I call you?" he said at the door.

"Of course," she said. "Thanks for a lovely dinner."

I'll call her then, he thought, going down in the elevator. It wasn't midnight yet, but most of L.A. was already asleep. His dark blue car was parked across Ocean Avenue with only one or two other cars now, where earlier that evening he'd been lucky to find the spot. It was a beautiful night, cool and clear but full of the scents of the nascent spring. I can call her, he thought, walking across the empty street, and wondered at the softness of the notion.

THE ACTRESS

For a year or so Elson had been acquainted with Steve Flores, a commercial filmmaker who made promotional and educational films as well as local TV commercials. Where had they met? He hadn't sold him a car. A Miata was too small for him; he was married with children still at home and Miatas were for divorced guys, such as himself, or otherwise single ones or stylish career women.

Flores came by the showroom one afternoon and asked him if he could take a break.

"You want to talk to me about this red convertible, right?"

"Please don't tempt me," he said. He was a good-looking, affable guy, he guessed a few years younger than he was.

"Starbucks?"

"Great. I won't keep you. I know you're at work."

They walked across the street, ordered macchiatos, and sat down in the all but empty, half-dark, coffee-redolent room.

"So what's up?"

"Well, I admire you," Steve said smiling. "You know that."

"My salesmanship."

"No, man," he said. "We all do what we have to do. I told you I caught your act at Largo years ago."

He remembered very well that Flores had said he'd heard him sing and only wanted to hear him say it again.

"Okay, well..." Flores said. "What I'm getting at here..." he went on in a sociable sing-song. "What I'm getting at... is...I'm doing a little play in your neighborhood, and—you're perfect for it."

It caught him by surprise, as if his other lifetime were trying him on for size again.

Two evenings later, he met Flores and the leading lady, Amy Church, who was an L.A. actress. She was standing on the stage in the theater around the corner from Elson's apartment when he arrived. She was quite tall and was wearing a sleeveless dark blue dress.

"Okay, people," Flores said from an aisle seat in the empty theater. "Let's read this sucker, shall we?"

It was a funny little play about a couple of actors, a woman and a man, who after an audition go to her apartment in Hollywood and a romance ensues in three scenes over the course of the night and the following morning—like a duet, masculine and feminine, a musical trade-off, and he began to get into it, sitting in the chair on the bare stage opposite Amy in a chair five or six feet away.

Every so often Steve would laugh. Then, 30 minutes or so into it, Elson realized she was playing certain notes that made Steve happy and his part was a kind of vamping behind her.

"I need a break," he said a minute or two later.

"Great," Steve said, standing up at his seat. "You guys are great together."

Jerry looked over at her, smiling and flushed.

Over the next three weeks of rehearsal, it was as if he were getting baptized into the dynamics of doing theater. Although he'd done small roles on television and in movies, the theater was much more like a real exploration of what acting was about.

The charge of Amy's performance might have had something to do with Steve in the audience, and Elson was on the other side of it, so that instead of a duet, it was some kind of trio. If it wasn't exactly the Jerry Elson Trio, it was something.

"You guys are great together," Steve said one night after his wife Esther arrived at the end of a rehearsal.

That night he and Amy ended up walking up Main Street for a coffee.

They got decaf cappuccinos and sat down at an outside table at The Daily Grind. As usual at the end of a rehearsal he felt shot up with psychological holes and at the same time exhilarated.

"I seem to be a little out of it sometimes," he said.

"Good!" she said and beamed at him.

"Why 'good'?"

"Because that's good for your performance. Don't you know that?"

"I guess I half-know it."

"That's good too."

It was a quiet Thursday night getting down into the sixties.

"He's a good guy," he said about Steve. A homeless woman walked by with a purposeful stride, heading down the hill.

They noticed her and Amy smiled.

"It's too bad he's married," she said. "Some girls have all the luck."

"You really want to be married."

"Why do you say it like that?"

"Because you're a good-looking thirtysomething actor and if you're not married it's probably because you don't want to be."

"How do you know I'm not married?"

For a moment the street was like a stage set with no particular audience and he realized he was ready or almost ready for sleep.

Opening night the audience was like a series of explosions that the two of them kept igniting. It was like the role played by Steve was replaced by 80 plus souls, some of whom Jerry recognized without actually knowing them.

"They love it," Steve whispered to them when the lights went down between the first two scenes.

When the lights came up again he was locked into his role and could do no wrong and so Amy seemed to feel across the flood lights. There were no real thoughts while he acted—but he could feel her energy, coming at him at various velocities, until he turned it around, with the audience punctuating each return, often with its laughter.

"Have fun, kids," Steve said when it went dark again before the last scene. "It doesn't get any better."

The reviewers in the local press indicated they liked what happened.

His fellow salesmen, Ruben Pacheco and Jason MacIntyre, attended a performance and MacIntyre was smitten by Amy.

"That's one fine woman, Jerry," he told him in the break room the next day. "You're involved, right?"

"No way," he said, sitting on the sofa with the L.A. Times while Jason browsed naked women on the iMac.

"You expect me to believe that?"

"I'm flattered you thought it was so believable, but we're acting. It's theater. If we were actually involved, we probably couldn't do it."

"Jesus, this chick is sick," he said. "I'm getting turned off this website. A lot of these women are exhibitionists."

They closed after a month, as scheduled. Steve Flores wandered into the showroom a couple of weeks later in mid-afternoon.

"Starbucks?" he said.

"Great."

In order to do the play, he'd been burning the candle at both ends and was still catching up. They sat down in the half-dark room with their macchiatos again.

"Man, I'm weary," Steve said.

"Hey, you did it!" he said. "I'm famous around here. I owe you everything."

"Thanks. I guess." He sighed.

"What?"

"Oh, man," Steve said. "I just almost lost it."

"Lost what?"

"Everything, man. My marriage. The theater is *way* too exciting."

"You're telling me you had an affair."

"No," he said. "And let's leave it at that, okay."

"Sure."

After rehearsing or performing the play for the better part of two months, turning inside out for each other every time they performed it, Jerry hadn't spoken to Amy, even on the phone, since they closed.

"Where's Amy these days?"

"I don't know," Steve said. "I'm married, man."

"I know you are..."

"So, anyway," Steve said. "How are you, man?"

TEETH

ELSON HAD SWITCHED DENTISTS WHEN HE'D moved from Thousand Oaks to the apartment in Ventura after the divorce was finalized and the house sold, but after several years the dentist, a sporty fifty-year-old who liked to scuba dive, decided to retire early and notified his patients in a nicely worded letter that Jerry couldn't help resent—the man was only fifty years old—recommending his office mate as his replacement. The transition would be seamless, but Elson thought he should probably move on. The office hygienist left something to be desired, he felt, even while he was tempted to ask her out. When she cleaned his teeth, it was as if they'd just made love and she had laid her upper body against his chest.

"Turn just a little this way, please," she said during the Wednesday afternoon appointment.

He turned.

"Thank you."

She had a son who was ten, and Jerry guessed the boy might benefit from a male presence, but then it occurred to him that he probably already had a few in his orbit who were courting his mother. Her name was Serena, a perfectly nice name. Why was he so critical of her? It was like a resistance in him, a lack of psychological space. Susie had left huge files in him that he had yet to move into the garbage. Maybe he never would. They had been young together. They had been beautiful. In any case, it didn't feel right to hit on the dental hygienist when his teeth didn't even seem very clean after his cleaning.

After the appointment he walked down Main Street. His apartment was on Palm, a few blocks down and half a block east toward the hills. It was that hour of late afternoon sunlight when everything had a permeable aspect. He would have to find another dentist, then, so his teeth would last a little longer. Serena needed a man and didn't really have time to focus on teeth past a certain professional threshold. On his side, it was his mouth, not his heart that needed commitment.

He passed the Second Time Around bookstore, where they had recently shot part of a Travolta movie. Hang out anywhere and show business arrived, but then it eventually went away. A parable about his career? He went across the street to see who was playing at Nicholby's. It was the usual interchangeable blues coalition, this one known as Lost in Time.

It struck him that there might be some telling comment embedded in the fact that while he'd spent decades as a professional singer, his primary health issue was his mouth. At the height of the sixties, when he was considered a total square for loving Jerome Kern and Harold Arlen, running a close second as an out-of-the-loop anomaly to Frank Sinatra, Jr.—his mouth, despite his living a rigorous organic life with Susie in Point Reyes Station, was giving out on him tooth by tooth.

The two of them were such purists that they didn't even own a bottle of Bufferin.

One night a back molar went ballistic on him. He wasn't sure how much more he could stand in the way of pain and Point Reyes was by now long-closed except for the bar, which he stepped into at most once or twice a year. He couldn't go next door, either, since he had no contact with his neighbor and harbored the suspicion that she was running an easy-come-easy-go, one-woman brothel.

In the middle of the pitch-black night, on their little street a short distance from the main drag, he tried virtually everything he could think of in the way of pain mitigation, including Zen sitting meditation and standing on his head. Nothing worked. Unable to sleep, he left their bedroom for the colorful living room graced with Susie's home-sewn slipcovers, sporadically engaging the idyll of having his head chopped off.

After unlocking the door of his second-floor-rear two-bedroom Ventura apartment, he walked in and sat down on the same sofa they'd had in their Point Reyes living room (Susie had picked up a new one at Ethan Allen and then moved with it to Simi Valley) and took off his shoes.

At six, that long-ago morning in Point Reyes, he got into their Volvo and drove to San Rafael. Cars were, he'd realized, sound-proof isolation chambers, allowing him the option of screaming, unthinkable at home with Susie and Todd asleep. Now he let go for all he was worth. Not long ago, John Lennon had done an album in Arthur Janov's primal scream idiom.

The screaming did little for him, although while the noise vibrated through his cranium it half-obliterated the pain, but the next moment the pain returned. A Rexall in San Rafael opened at seven o'clock. After waiting in his car until the door was unlocked, he bought a bottle of Bufferin and went for breakfast at the French Coffee Shop on Fifth Street. He had the special of eggs, bacon, home fries, toast and coffee, having taken two Bufferin early on with his water.

Within fifteen minutes, as he read the *San Francisco Chronicle*, the pain, the terrible pain he'd known all night, was somehow in harness, and then it was gone. Gone! It was clear to him that the inventor of Bufferin was entitled to the Nobel Prize.

Shoes off, he lay down on the sofa and looked out his back window at a willow tree, a tree that hovered over a brick patio used by the local theater during intermission. They were doing something by Pinter these days and he thought he ought to drop by one of these evenings. He'd been dating Nancy Spears. It was a year or so after high school that they'd gotten together and it was the sense that he could do anything in Nancy's presence—and she would only laugh and encourage him and enjoy it—that quickly drove him away, eventually to Susie, who brought a complementary, if not always compliant energy to their relationship.

Nancy was probably a certifiable sex maniac, while he was some sort of dyed-in-the-wool Puritan. A couple of times over the years, he'd had dreams about getting sexual favors from Nancy when things were running down with Susie, and the other night he'd woken up in Nancy's bed.

"What are you doing?" he said.

"What do you think I'm doing?"

"Nancy, we're in our fifties…Aren't we?"

"What's that supposed to mean?"

He was having more orgasms than he was used to and it was making him tired at work. On the other hand, worse things could happen to you.

Lying on the living room sofa, he thought he should call her.

"Do you want to rent *Eyes Wide Shut*?" she'd asked on the latest voicemail.

"Let me ask you something?"

"Yes?" she said.

"Do you really think we're going to have a good time watching this?"

"Well…" she said. He was looking at the living room wall with the framed poster of Botticelli's "Three Graces" he'd bought at the Z Gallery one afternoon in Santa Barbara when he was missing Susie. It was a very beautiful painting—perhaps the most beautiful ever painted—and one of the graces reminded him of Susie.

He didn't say anything.

"Tell me something you love about me," Nancy said.

"I like the way you dance."

"Have we danced together?"

"I meant you move as though you're dancing sometimes."

"Really? That's nice," she said. "Okay, you get a treat."

"What is it?"

"You have to get here to find out."

POSTSCRIPT

THE SOUND OF LOVE

One evening in late Spring—right after daylight savings time, so it was light again till almost eight at night—Carol and Walter, neither of whom had a job at the moment, were walking down Fifty-seventh Street and past the Great Northern Hotel, where Carol knew Bill liked to stay. (He had written The Time Of Your Life there in six days and kept his warm associations with the place even as it declined.) As they headed east toward the corner of Sixth Avenue, approaching the Automat in the middle of the block, she was about to remark to Walter that Bill always liked to eat at the Automat, when suddenly she saw her ex-husband sitting with another man at one of the tables in the picture window at the front of the cafeteria.

"Oh my God, I think that's Bill."

"In the Automat?"

"Yes—oh don't look! He'll see us."

"Sweetheart, he's your ex-husband. Not an SS officer."

"Oh, you're right, darling," she said, holding Walter's arm tighter and picking up her pace, "But do me a favor and don't look."

"Whatever you say, pussycat."

They continued toward the corner of Sixth Avenue, the evening sky still blue through the wide corridor of Fifty-seventh Street. They passed a construction sight, closed up for the day.

"When I was young," Walter told her, "I used to like to watch the fellas working—whatta they call em? People who watch the men working?

"Transients?"

Walter laughed his silent, appreciative laugh.

As they approached the corner, Carol began to unclench from the near encounter with Bill. Then, just as she was feeling safely beyond his orbit, there he was, along with another man, perhaps the one he'd been sitting with at the Automat, walking briskly up Sixth Avenue, from the direction of Fifty-sixth Street, toward them,

"Well," Bill said in his booming voice, as their paths were about to cross, and with a jovial look at the two of them, "if you walk around New York long enough, sooner or later you meet your family."

"Hiya, Bill," Walter said to him smiling.

"Hello, Walter, old buddy."

"Hello, Bill." She made herself simple. It was absurd, but she suddenly felt rather calm.

"Well, it's a beautiful evening for a walk."

"Yes, it is," she answered.

Let him work this one out.

"I'm going to call the kids. I just got into town."

"Wonderful."

"All right, now, you two have a good walk. Dickran and I have some very important business to attend to right down the street here at the Automat. Right, Dickran?"

The man, a small, compact Armenian with a dour look, brightened slightly and replied, "Right, Bill."

They continued on their way.

"Don't tell me you think I'm crazy," Carol said to Walter on the other side of Sixth Avenue, "I swear to you it was him in the window of the Automat."

"Oh, no," Walter told her as Carol slowed down to look at pocketbooks in Bendel's windows, "I believe you. I think maybe Bill still cares about you. Jesus, he must have made that guy hustle to get all the way around the block like that."

Carol giggled, "Oh, I can just see him making that poor man run."

"But what I want to know—" Walter went on, as they picked up the pace again, "—what I want to know is what do they call those people who watch them work at construction sites?"

"Bums?"

Walter laughed again without laughing out loud. They continued then, arm and arm, to the corner of Fifth Avenue.

"Loiterers," he said suddenly, breaking a silence neither had noticed.

"They call them loiterers. Remember that one for your writing. It's a good one for your vocabulary."

"Oh, I will, darling. Don't worry. I will."

ACKNOWLEDGMENTS

Grateful acknowledgment is made to the editors and publishers of the following publications, in which parts of this book first appeared: *Best American Poetry* blog (online), *Best Buddhist Writing 2004* (Shambhala Books, 2005), *First of the Month* (online), *Los Angeles Times Sunday Magazine, Markaz Review* (online), and *Shambhala Sun.*

ABOUT THE AUTHOR

Aram Saroyan is a poet and author best known for his minimalist poems. His *Complete Minimal Poems* received the 2008 William Carlos Williams Award from the Poetry Society of America. He is featured in the documentary film *One Quick Move or I'm Gone: Jack Kerouac at Big Sur* and his comments appear in the oral biographies *George Being George: George Plimpton's Life* and *Salinger.* He is the author of *Still Night in L.A.*, *Trio,* and the true crime Literary Guild selection *Rancho Mirage,* as well as many other books of prose and poetry. He lives in Las Vegas.

RECENT AND FORTHCOMING BOOKS FROM THREE ROOMS PRESS

FICTION

Lucy Jane Bledsoe
No Stopping Us Now

Rishab Borah
The Door to Inferna

Meagan Brothers
Weird Girl and What's His Name

Christopher Chambers
Scavenger
Standalone
StreetWhys

Ebele Chizea
Aquarian Dawn

Heather Colley
The Gilded Butterfly Effect

Ron Dakron
Hello Devilfish!

Ron Dakron
Hello Devilfish!

Robert Duncan
Loudmouth

Amanda Eisenberg
People Are Talking

Michael T. Fournier
Hidden Wheel
Swing State

Kate Gale
Under a Neon Sun

Aaron Hamburger
Nirvana Is Here

William Least Heat-Moon
Celestial Mechanics

Aimee Herman
Everything Grows

Kelly Ann Jacobson
Tink and Wendy
Robin and Her Misfits
Lies of the Toymaker

Jethro K. Lieberman
Everything Is Jake

Eamon Loingsigh
Light of the Diddicoy
Exile on Bridge Street

John Marshall
The Greenfather

Alvin Orloff
Vulgarian Rhapsody

Micki Janae
Of Blood and Lightning

Aram Saroyan
Still Night in L.A.

Robert Silverberg
The Face of the Waters

Stephen Spotte
Animal Wrongs

Max Talley
Peace, Love and Haight

Richard Vetere
The Writers Afterlife
Champagne and Cocaine

Jessamyn Violet
Secret Rules to Being a Rockstar

Julia Watts
Quiver
Needlework
Lovesick Blossoms

Gina Yates
Narcissus Nobody

MEMOIR & BIOGRAPHY

Nassrine Azimi and Michel Wasserman
Last Boat to Yokohama: The Life and Legacy of Beate Sirota Gordon

William S. Burroughs & Allen Ginsberg
Don't Hide the Madness
edited by Steven Taylor

James Carr
BAD: The Autobiography of James Carr

Judy Gumbo
Yippie Girl: Exploits in Protest and Defeating the FBI

Nancy Kurshan
Levitating the Pentagon and Other Uplifting Stories

Hédi A. Jaouad
The Immortal Journeys of Isabelle Eberhardt

Judith Malina
Full Moon Stages: Personal Notes from 50 Years of The Living Theatre

Phil Marcade
Punk Avenue: Inside the New York City Underground, 1972–1982

Jillian Marshall
Japanthem: Counter-Cultural Experiences; Cross-Cultural Remixes

Alvin Orloff
Disasterama! Adventures in the Queer Underground 1977–1997

Angelica Page
A Delicious Life: Growing Up with Geraldine Page
Ray by Ray: A Daughter's Take on the Legend of Nicholas Ray

Nicca Ray
Ray by Ray: A Daughter's Take on the Legend of Nicholas Ray

Aram Saroyan
Before I Forget: A Memoir

Stephen Spotte
My Watery Self: Memoirs of a Marine Scientist

Christina Vo & Nghia M. Vo
My Vietnam, Your Vietnam
Vietnamese translation: *Việt Nam Của Con, Việt Nam Của Cha*

PHOTOGRAPHY-MEMOIR

Mike Watt
On & Off Bass

DADA

Maintenant: A Journal of Contemporary Dada Writing & Art (annual, since 2008)

MIXED MEDIA

John S. Paul
Sign Language: A Painter's Notebook (photography, poetry and prose)

HUMOR

Peter Carlaftes
A Year on Facebook

FILM & PLAYS

Israel Horovitz
My Old Lady: Complete Stage Play and Screenplay with an Essay on Adaptation

Peter Carlaftes
Triumph For Rent (3 Plays)
Teatrophy (3 More Plays)

Kat Georges
Three Somebodies: Plays

TRANSLATIONS

Thomas Bernhard
On Earth and in Hell
(poems; German and English)

Patrizia Gattaceca
Isula d'Anima (Corsican & English)

César Vallejo | Gerard Malanga
Malanga Chasing Vallejo

George Wallace
EOS: Abductor of Men (Greek & English)

ESSAYS

Richard Katrovas
Raising Girls in Bohemia

Vanessa Baden Kelly
Far Away From Close to Home

Erin Wildermuth
Womentality

SHORT STORY ANTHOLOGIES

SINGLE AUTHOR

Alien Archives: Stories
by Robert Silverberg

First-Person Singularities: Stories
by Robert Silverberg

Tales from the Eternal Café: Stories
by Janet Hamill, intro by Patti Smith

Time and Time Again: Sixteen Trips in Time
by Robert Silverberg

The Unvarnished Gary Phillips: A Mondo Pulp Collection
by Gary Phillips

Voyagers: Twelve Journeys in Space and Time
by Robert Silverberg

MULTI-AUTHOR

The Colors of April
edited by Quan Manh Ha & Cab Tran

Crime + Music: Nineteen Stories of Music-Themed Noir
edited by Jim Fusilli

Dark City Lights: New York Stories
edited by Lawrence Block

The Faking of the President: Twenty Stories of White House Noir
edited by Peter Carlaftes

Florida Happens:
edited by Greg Herren

Have a NYC I, II & III: New York Stories;
edited by Peter Carlaftes & Kat Georges

Songs of My Selfie
edited by Constance Renfrow

The Obama Inheritance: 15 Stories of Conspiracy Noir
edited by Gary Phillips

This Way to the End Times: Classic & New Stories of the Apocalypse
edited by Robert Silverberg

POETRY COLLECTIONS

Hala Alyan
Atrium

Peter Carlaftes
DrunkYard Dog
I Fold with the Hand I Was Dealt
Life in the Past Lane

Thomas Fucaloro
It Starts from the Belly and Blooms

Kat Georges
Our Lady of the Hunger
Awe and Other Words Like Wow

Robert Gibbons
Close to the Tree

Israel Horovitz
Heaven and Other Poems

David Lawton
Sharp Blue Stream

Jane LeCroy
Signature Play

Philip Meersman
This Is Belgian Chocolate

Jane Ormerod
Recreational Vehicles on Fire
Welcome to the Museum of Cattle

Lisa Panepinto
On This Borrowed Bike

George Wallace
Poppin' Johnny

www.ingramcontent.com/pod-product-compliance
Lightning Source LLC
Jackson TN
JSHW020005100326
98977JS00009B/920

* 9 7 8 1 9 5 3 1 0 3 6 8 0 *